Bold Women in Alaska History

MARJORIE COCHRANE

2014
Mountain Press Publishing Company
Missoula, Montana

Library of Congress Cataloging-in-Publication Data

Cochrane, Marjorie.
 Bold women in Alaska history / Marjorie Cochrane.
    pages cm. – (Bold women series)
 Includes bibliographical references and index.
 ISBN 978-0-87842-617-1 (paperback : alkaline paper)
 1. Women–Alaska–Biography–Juvenile literature. 2. Women heroes–
Alaska–Biography–Juvenile literature. 3. Women–Alaska–History–
Juvenile literature. 4. Alaska–Biography–Juvenile literature. 5. Alaska–
History–Juvenile literature. I. Title.
 CT3262.A4C63 2014
 920.7209798–dc23
                           2014014828

PRINTED IN THE UNITED STATES

MP Mountain Press
PUBLISHING COMPANY
P.O. Box 2399 • Missoula, MT 59806 • 406-728-1900
800-234-5308 • info@mtnpress.com
www.mountain-press.com

To my mother, Karen, and my Aunt Irene,
two of the boldest women I've known

Acknowledgments

When editor Gwen McKenna first called to see if I'd like to write a book about Alaska's bold women, of course I said YES! I have loved delving into the lives of these eleven intriguing ladies, through what they've written and what has been written about them. In several of the biographies, family members have been kind enough to share their memories with me. I owe special thanks to Nora Guinn's daughter Susan Murphy; to Elizabeth Peratrovich's son Roy Peratrovich, Jr.; to Thelma Buccholdt's husband, Jon Buccholdlt; and to Mahala Dickerson's son John. Additionally, it was a joy to get to meet Mary Shields herself through phone calls and e-mails and to learn from her about her life.

I had help as well from former Chugiak-Eagle River Star editor Lee Jordan, always a source of information about all things Alaskan, as well as from Jon Van Zyle, Sylvia Short, Maxine Rader, and Kay Wieman.

Editor Gwen has double-checked facts, added research, hunted up photos, and kept my writing focused on the lives of the women rather than wandering too far afield. This is as much her book as mine and I am most appreciative.

Finally, to my five children, Becky, Ann, Cathy, Nancy, and Andrew, and their spouses: thank you for always being my loving and most enthusiastic critics!

Contents

1. Natalia Shelikhova
2. Mary Antisarlook
3. Rusty Dow
4. Barrett Willoughby
5. Elizabeth Peratrovich
6. Mahala Ashley Dickerson
7. Celia Hunter and Ginny Hill Wood
8. Nora Guinn
9. Thelma Buchholdt
10. Mary Shields

BEAUFORT SEA

CHUKCHI SEA

RUSSIA

CANADA
U.S.A.

YUKON TERRITORY

ALASKA

Barrow

Point Hope

Kotzebue 7

SEWARD PENINSULA
Teller 8
Port Clarence 2
Sinuk (Sinrock)
Nome 10

St. Michael 2

Marshall 8

Akiak 8

Bethel

Tununak 8

NELSON ISLAND

BERING SEA

ALEUTIAN ISLANDS

UNIMAK ISLAND

BRISTOL BAY

Rampart

Fairbanks 7 10

DENALI NATIONAL PARK 7

Dawson City 4

Skagway

Juneau 9 4 5
Sitka 5 1
Klawock 5
Petersburg 5
Wrangell 4 5
Ketchikan 5

Katalla 4

MIDDLETON ISLAND

GULF OF ALASKA

Palmer 6 3
Eklutna 8
Wasilla 6 3
ANCHORAGE 10 9 6 4 3
Seward 4
KENAI NATIONAL PARK 10
Kenai 6 4 3

KATMAI NATIONAL PARK 7

Kodiak 4 1
Old Harbor 1
(Three Saints Bay)

N

0 250 500 miles
0 250 500 kilometers

Introduction

In a way, all women who live in Alaska are bold, especially those who lived there in its early days. Choosing only eleven of them to represent the achievements of women in Alaska's history was a difficult task. This book contains only a sampling of the many courageous women who not only survived in this remote and rugged place, but indeed made it a better place to live for everyone.

These eleven women lived in different ages, from the Russian era of the 1700s to the twenty-first century. They also came from different ethnicities, including black, white, Filipino, Tlingit, and Yu'pik Eskimo. Most of these women came to Alaska from elsewhere, but three—Mary Antisarlook, Elizabeth Peratrovich, and Nora Guinn—were born here. Some came from wealthy families, while others had middle-class or even impoverished backgrounds. All but Celia Hunter were married at least once, and three of the women had several husbands during their lives. Natalia Shelikhova and Nora Guinn had large families; both also adopted or took care of other children as well. Mary Antisarlook had no children of her own but adopted many orphans over the course of her life. Others—Rusty Dow, Barrett Willoughby, Celia Hunter, and Mary Shields—had no children. All had careers, ranging from reindeer herder to district court judge, from truck driver to political activist, from pilot to novelist, and from dog musher to legislator. Whatever their field of endeavor, all made an indelible mark on the Last Frontier.

Arranging these biographies in the order of the women's year of birth, we begin with Natalia Shelikhova. Natalia was not only the first white woman in Alaska, she also acted as the territory's first governor when her husband, Grigorii, was traveling. In addition, she help manage her husband's fur company and later started a school for Aleut children. After Grigorii's death, Natalia established the Russian-American Company and obtained a monopoly for its Alaskan commerce.

Next is Mary Antisarlook, "Reindeer Mary." Half Russian, half Inupiaq Eskimo, Mary managed her own reindeer herd near Nome during the gold-rush days and gained fame as the wealthiest woman in Alaska. Noted for her generosity, she used her wealth to help the community, adopting eleven children and caring for countless others.

Benzie "Rusty" Scott Dow, having grown up driving a truck on her family's farm, took her driving skills—and her truck—to the Matanuska Valley in the late 1930s and started a transportation service. During World War II, she proved herself as a driver and was selected to make the first-ever round trip over the new Alaska-Canadian (Alcan) Highway, a distance of more than 1,500 miles each way. After the war, she and her husband, Russ Dow, homesteaded north of Anchorage. Rusty's self-taught artistic abilities also brought her recognition.

Barrett Willoughby, born Florence Barrett, grew up aboard her parents' sailboat and fell in love with Alaska at an early age. Wanting to share the Last Frontier's mystery and beauty, she wrote romantic novels with Alaskan settings that became national best-sellers in the 1920s and 1930s. Her books and articles helped convince the American public that there was much more to Alaska than snow and ice.

Elizabeth Wanamaker Peratrovich, of Tlingit heritage, was raised by adoptive parents in the fishing villages of southeastern Alaska. She and her husband Roy Peratrovich were active in the Alaska Native Brotherhood and Sisterhood. It was Elizabeth's speaking ability and lobbying efforts that led the Alaska legislature to pass the nation's first antidiscrimination bill in 1945.

Mahala Ashley Dickerson, who grew up in Alabama, faced the widespread discrimination of the pre-civil-rights South. Mahala eventually overcame this racism to become Alabama's first African American woman lawyer. After moving to Alaska, she became the first black homesteader in the Matanuska Valley and the first African American to be admitted to the Alaska Bar Association. As an attorney, Mahala represented Anchorage's poorest and most victimized citizens.

Celia Hunter and Ginny Hill, the subjects of our dual biography, were both pilots during World War II. At war's end, curious to see Alaska, the two flew a pair of war-surplus planes to Fairbanks in midwinter. What began as an adventure became a lifelong devotion to Alaska. Loving the wilderness of Mount McKinley (Denali) National Park, Celia and Ginny, along with Ginny's husband Morton "Woody" Wood, established Camp Denali, a rustic camp where visitors could enjoy the wilderness around them. Soon the two friends became involved in statewide conservation efforts, including the creation of the Arctic National Wildlife Range.

Nora Venes Guinn was born in a Yu'pik Eskimo community in the Yukon-Kuskokwim Delta. After graduating from high school, she married Charlie Guinn and eventually settled in Bethel, where they raised their nine children and opened their home to numerous others. In Bethel, Nora served as a territorial commissioner, then a magistrate, and finally a district court judge; she was the first Native Alaskan and one of the very few non-lawyers ever to hold that office. The courthouse in Bethel was named for her in recognition of the understanding she offered Native Alaskans in the courtroom.

Thelma Garcia Buchholdt was born in the Philippines and as a child endured the Japanese occupation of that nation during World War II. An uncle brought her to Los Angeles to attend college, and before she was able to return to the Philippines she met her future husband, Jon Buchholdt. Thelma and Jon later moved to Anchorage, where Thelma's skills in community organizing led to her election to the Alaska House of Representatives, making her the first female Filipino-American legislator in the nation. During her four terms, Thelma worked to address environmental concerns in Alaska. She was also active in the Filipino community in Anchorage and eventually wrote a book about the role Filipinos played in Alaska's history.

Our final chapter focuses on Mary Shields, pioneer Iditarod racer and dog musher extraordinaire. Mary, the only one of our subjects who is still living at the time of publication, welcomes visitors to her homestead each summer, showing guests around the property, introducing them to her sled dogs, and demonstrating sledding techniques. In addition, she has written a number of books about her life and her passion for the wilderness, for sledding, and for dogs.

The eleven women portrayed here were indeed bold—breaking down barriers of sexism, racial prejudice, and political opposition to emerge as heroines of their time. We hope that you will not only enjoy their stories, but will also be inspired by them to become a little bolder yourself.

NATALIA SHELIKHOVA

Alaska's First Woman Governor

Late in 1783, sailing under the Russian flag, three merchant ships, called galiots, were struggling eastward through perilous waters. The expedition had set sail in August from Okhotsk, on the Russian coast, where the ships had been built. The voyagers' destination was the island of Kodiak, off the Alaskan coast, more than 2,000 miles away. After rounding the Kamchatka Peninsula, they were now facing ferocious storms in the northern Pacific Ocean.

The ships carried nearly two hundred workers and tons of supplies. The goal of the expedition was to establish the first permanent trading post and settlement in Russian America (Alaska) for the Shelikhov-Golikov fur-trading company. Russia had claimed the lands of Alaska in 1733, but the territory had remained largely unsettled.

Aboard the leading galiot, named the *Three Saints*, were expedition leader Grigorii Shelikhov, his young wife Natalia Shelikhova, and their one-year-old son Mikhail. An experienced seafarer, Grigorii Shelikhov is sometimes called "Russia's Columbus," as he would discover much about the northernmost lands of the New World. Natalia would also make her way into history books, as she was the first white woman to set foot in Alaska. Moreover, after her husband's death, she took over the family's Alaskan fur-trading monopoly, giving her control of all Russian territory in North America—thus she came to be regarded as Russian Alaska's first female governor.

Natalia was not much more than a child when she caught the eye of trader Grigorii Shelikhov in Irkutsk, Siberia. At the time, Grigorii—son of a merchant from Rylsk, in south-central Russia, and a Russian noblewoman—was working in Irkutsk as a salesman for wine merchant Ivan Golikov. Golikov was planning to start a new business trading furs in Alaska, and before long he would ask the well-organized and ambitious Grigorii to be his partner in the new company. In the meantime, in Irkutsk, Grigorii commenced courting the young and lovely Natalia.

Natalia was born, probably in Irkutsk, in 1761. The names of her parents are uncertain, but her father may have been a navigator and mapmaker, which could account for Natalia's interest in far-away lands. In any case, her family is believed to have been fairly well-to-do, so she probably brought a sizable dowry to her marriage in 1775. When the couple wed, Natalia was about fourteen, a common age of marriage for Russian girls of that era, and Grigorii was about twenty-seven.

A year and a half later, Natalia gave birth to a son, called Ivan, but he died in infancy. In 1780 she had a daughter, Anna, and in 1781 she had another girl, Ekaterina, followed by son Mikhail in 1782. The two little girls were still toddlers when their parents left for Alaska. Grigorii and Natalia left their daughters in the care of relatives in Irkutz for the three years they expected to be gone, but they took little Mikhail with them.

To reach Kodiak Island was an ambitious goal. The Shelikhov expedition would be sailing on largely uncharted seas where few explorers had ventured successfully. Even to this day, ships are often lost in the vicious waters of the northern Pacific. Across the Bering

Sea stretched the 1,200-mile island chain known as the Aleutian Islands, with its seventy-six volcanoes, some of them active. Few of the islands were inhabited, so if they foundered, there would be no one to help them. From there, it was another 700 miles to Kodiak.

It was in these waters that Danish explorer Vitus Bering, working for the Russian emperor and sailing a Russian Navy ship, had been forced aground forty years earlier on his journey back from Alaska. Storms had driven his vessel ashore on the island that now bears his name—Bering Island, the largest of the Commander Islands.

While Bering had succeeded in exploring parts of Alaska for Russia, he did not make it back from this expedition. He died of an illness, probably scurvy, on the island. His crew, however, returned with news of a wealth of fur-bearing animals on the Aleutian Islands. The pelts of sea otters as well as those of fur seals, sea cows (later hunted to extinction), and foxes were greatly valued in the global marketplace of the eighteenth and early nineteenth centuries. The furs were used mostly for clothing, especially in China. The pelts that Bering's men brought back to Russia set off what could be called a "gold rush" to the Aleutians, with sea-otter skins being the gold.

As the fur rush to Alaska intensified, Russian traders hired hundreds of hunters, sailors, and navigators to go to the Aleutians for pelts. These hired men were called the promyshlenniki. To assist them, the promyshlenniki turned to the native islanders, the Aleuts, a seafaring people skilled at harvesting ocean animals. But the Russians weren't always nice about it. They often forced the Aleut men to hunt for them at gunpoint, taking their women and children hostage until the men returned with the pelts. Sometimes they brutalized the Aleuts and other Native peoples, even killing them. In a few cases, the islanders fought back, and over the years there were a number of bloody battles between Native Alaskans and the promyshlenniki. Ultimately, when the fur trade died down in the mid-1800s, the violence did too, but when Grigorii and Natalia

Shelikhov were making their way to Kodiak Island in 1784, the situation was still tense.

As the demand for furs continued to grow in the late 1700s, so did the number of companies competing for the business. Among these companies was the partnership of Grigorii Shelikhov and Ivan Golikov, established in 1781. The first few ships they sent to Alaska brought them good profits, but the otter population was already becoming severely diminished in some places, and it was difficult to manage harvests made thousands of miles from their headquarters in Irkutsk. To succeed in the long term, Grigorii realized, the company needed a permanent base in Alaska. He began to make preparations for building a settlement on Kodiak Island.

The costs involved were considerable. The Shelikhov-Golikov Company needed to borrow enough money to cover transportion, workers, food, and supplies not only for the expedition but also for establishing the colony. For that they would need building materials and tools, seeds and farming equipment, livestock and feed, guns, and other necessities. Natalia enthusiastically supported her husband's proposal and worked energetically to help him find investors. Some of the financing probably came from Natalia herself. Because education was important to her and to Grigorii, they agreed that the colony would include a school for Native children.

In the months preceding their departure, Grigorii spent much of his time in Okhotsk, more than 1,500 miles northeast of Irkutsk, to oversee the shipbuilding and preparations. Thus Natalia was left to manage his business interests in Irkutsk as well as taking care of the children and the household. She learned quickly and handled it all very competently. By the time they sailed, Natalia was pregnant with another child, but this did not deter her from taking the voyage to Alaska.

By October, the *Three Saints* and the other two galiots were struggling through the storms on the Bering Sea. After one of the ships disappeared somewhere in the towering waves (its crew and cargo were assumed lost, but the ship reappeared three years later), Grigorii decided it would be foolish to push their luck. The two surviving ships were close to the Commander Islands, the westernmost of the Aleutian Islands, where the travelers could find winter shelter. The expedition would have to wait until late spring to continue to their destination, still about 1,000 miles away. It was during their winter on Bering Island that the Shelikhovs' third daughter, Avdotia, was born. Her parents nicknamed her Amerikanka—"American girl."

When the weather looked good enough, probably around early June, the Shelikhov expedition resumed the voyage to Kodiak Island. Joining the colonists were some promyshlenniki who had been working in the Aleutians, along with their Aleut wives and children. By Russian law, the children of these unofficial marriages belonged to the mothers, and Aleut women were not permitted to live in Russia with their husbands. Some of the promyshlenniki deserted their families to return to Russia, but many stayed and spent the rest of their lives in Alaska.

The expedition finally reached Kodiak Island on August 3, 1784. After a cold and foggy winter in the barren Aleutians, the tree-covered mountains and milder climate of Kodiak must have been a welcome relief to the travelers. Grigorii selected a pleasant site on an inlet on the island's south shore for the new settlement, naming it Three Saints Bay (near today's Kodiak), after their ship. They anchored nearby to wait for the native islanders to appear before venturing ashore to begin building. Earlier promyshlenniki had warned them that the natives here, the Alutiiq, would be more hostile than the Aleuts had been. When their ships attempted to land there, the Russian hunters said, the Alutiiq had showered them with arrows and deflected their musket fire with hard breastplates and shields.

Indeed, shortly after the expedition landed, one of Grigorii's crew members said he believed that the natives were gathering at a high rocky islet on the coast and were planning an attack. Grigorii took most of his men and five cannons to investigate. He found the Alutiiq warriors and ordered his men to fire the cannons, killing an unknown number of islanders, who soon surrendered in the face of the Russians' superior fire power. The battle site is now called Refuge Rock. Many of the survivors were taken hostage and put to work. In spite of this harsh introduction, afterward Grigorii insisted that the natives be treated with fairness and kindness.

Over time, the Alutiiq gradually accepted the newcomers, and many even joined the Russian work crews on their own. In fact, the colonists befriended many of the natives, and Natalia took at least one, an Alutiiq woman called Ekaterina Merkuleva, as her goddaughter. The Russian Orthodox Church encouraged the adoption of both youngsters and adults, whether Russian or not, as godchildren. This practice introduced Christianity to the native Alaskans and helped the Russians bond with them. Natalia asked the church to send priests to their new settlement, to bless marriages and baptize children, but it would be eight years before the first ones arrived.

While Grigorii oversaw the settlement's construction, Natalia set up a store and took charge of handling the food and supplies, keeping individual records for each worker. According to their contracts, the promyshlenniki would receive a share in the company's profits, but the cost of their food and supplies would be deducted from the total. Natalia taught Ekaterina to help her manage the store and keep the records.

Within a year, Three Saints Bay included homes, barns, storage buildings, and blacksmith and carpentry shops. Gardens were planted with barley, beans, potatoes, beets, and other vegetables. The school that Natalia established was rudimentary but successful—she found the native and mixed-blood children to be eager learners. As the time approached for the Russians' planned departure, some of the

Engraving of Three Saints Bay, circa 1790, by artist Luka Voronin —Alaska State Library,
Wickersham State Historic Site Photographs Collection, ASL-P277-008-004

Alaskans asked the Shelikhovs to take their children back to Russia
be educated. They agreed. Among them were ten boys who would
receive musical training, five of them under the Shelikhovs' personal
care, and twelve other boys who would be trained as navigators.

By the spring of 1786, with their colony well established, the Shelikhovs were ready to return to Russia. Most of the promyshlenniki
remained in Alaska to continue harvesting furs, and Natalia left her
goddaughter Ekaterina Merkuleva in charge of the store. Then the
Shelikhovs, with their own two children and their native students,
sailed out of Three Saints Bay with a crew made up largely of Alutiiq natives. The *Three Saints* arrived safely in Kamchatka on August
8, 1786. From there they went home to Irkutz.

Sadly, not long after the Shelikhovs' return, their young son Mikhail died. A new baby boy was born shortly after his brother's death, but he lived only a few months. The causes of the deaths were not recorded, but in those days deadly illnesses were common, especially among children, and medical care was seldom effective or even available.

In spite of their personal grief, Grigorii and Natalia continued tending to their business interests. Their description of what they had accomplished in Alaska impressed the governor-general of Eastern Siberia so much that he wrote to Empress Catherine II recommending that she grant the Shelikhov-Golikov company a monopoly of trading rights in North America. He suggested to Natalia and Grigorii that they and their partner Ivan Golikov go to the Russian capital, St. Petersburg, to present the recommendation in person. Eager to get a personal audience with Catherine the Great, they prepared for the journey to St. Petersburg, where they hoped they could also obtain a loan to expand their trade with Japan and the western Pacific.

Optimistic, the Shelikhovs left by horse-drawn sleigh in December 1787, traversing some 3,700 miles of ice- and snow-covered subarctic forest. Once they reached St. Petersburg, however, they found that it would be many months before they could get a meeting with the empress. Nevertheless, the Shelikhovs were treated well and received introductions to some of the nobles in Catherine's court. Natalia must have enjoyed the glamour and luxury of the capital city after enduring the difficulties and deprivations of life in Alaska. While in St. Petersburg, Natalia discovered that she was again pregnant. It was an exhilarating time.

In the end, the empress denied the Shelikhovs' request for a monopoly, but she did reward Grigorii and his partner Ivan Golikov with imperial gold medals and silver sabers, a sign of a high social position. In the late fall of 1788, Natalia and Grigorii left for the long trip back to Irkutz. Historians believe that their fourth daughter, Aleksandra, was probably born on the journey, during a stop in Moscow or Kylsk.

Shortly after the Shelikhovs got home, Grigorii had to leave again for Okhotsk to oversee the outfitting of more ships to send to Three Saints Bay. Over the next several years, he would be away from home at least six months each year. While he was gone, Natalia again took charge of the fur company's business. The letters she wrote to Grigorii during his lengthy absences (translated by Dawn Lea Black and Alexander Yu. Petrov) provide glimpses of her hectic life operating a business, running a household, and raising children.

The first summer without her husband, 1789, was particularly challenging for Natalia—in addition to her numerous other duties, she was responsible for supervising the music students the Shelikhovs had brought to Irkutsk from Alaska. These boys would later be sent back to Kodiak Island in order to bring Russian culture to the colony there.

Natalia handled everything remarkably well. In managing the business, she paid close attention to the quality of the furs she received and was competitive in seeking top prices. She also oversaw the goods the company received in trade. In one letter, she complained that a sugar shipment she had received was not of good quality and that a shipment of wine was short a few bottles. In addition, she supervised shipments of supplies to Alaska; one such load included "nails, bolts, candles, soap, oak flasks and shoes." Several letters reveal Natalia's self-assurance as a manager: "I was informed that big swindlers are swindling people here. I have been biding my time for now but will crack down on them forcefully." She was just as stringent regarding the household, assuring Grigorii that "I keep all the domestic workers in the house under strict control."

Naturally, Natalia's letters were full of news about their children. Shortly after Grigorii left in 1789, she wrote proudly of their four girls, "Our children are writing, and the teachers are happy that God bestowed such children on us." Later, two more girls and two boys would join the family, though as with the Shelikhovs' previous children, not all of them would live to adulthood.

Natalia's concern for the Kodiak boys they were educating in music, as well as in religion and the Russian language, is often expressed in her letters. In late May 1789 she wrote that all five boys, as well as their daughter Aleksandra, had been ill with "fits of coughing, diarrhea, and vomiting." One of them, Attaku, was "really sick after your departure and he is still sick." She called a doctor to treat them. "It has been very difficult." Of the Native Alaskan boys she said, "I think I will have them baptized, all of them, because they already agreed to this."

The children had all recovered by early June and were able to resume their schooling. "We have started to teach the Americans [Native Alaskans] the alphabet and to play musical instruments. They are studying well. . . . Only Andrei is not good at understanding but even he has started to understand." Apparently Andrei (Andriushka) did not improve as much as Natalia expected, for a month later she wrote, "I visited the Americans yesterday. . . . Andriushka does not understand well how to play the bass. The teacher has spanked him twice and if he can't understand I will make a decision to leave him out and not teach him anymore." The other boys were doing fine, though. "Fedka plays the flute well. Three [of the boys] . . . play the violin really well."

Sadly, however, in July, one of the Native boys, Attaka, had again become sick with a diarrheal illness, and about two weeks later he died. "He wanted to be baptized and passed away the very same day."

Happier news came in 1791, when Natalia gave birth to a boy named Vasilii, nicknamed Vasenka. Many of her letters tell of his progress—Vasenka is starting to walk, Vasenka is running, Vasenka needs boots from St. Petersburg. Natalia often asked Grigorii to bring back items for the family, such as "good and fashionable hats" for her and the girls, as well as "two strings of the best pearls [and] a pretty snuffbox for myself." Another letter requested "two pieces of printed cotton with a few colors, one hat and one buckle for Vasenka." The children had their own wish lists for school supplies: "We humbly ask you to buy us four books, a general geography, a Russian one with maps, a brief one with maps and an atlas with maps. All these are for our studies."

Meanwhile, back in Alaska, Three Saints Bay's new manager, Aleksander Baranov, was busy rebuilding. Grigorii had hired Baranov in 1790, but Baranov's ship had capsized on the way and he did not make his way to Kodiak Island until the following year. He

Sign in front of Baranof (Baranov) House Museum in Kodiak. This 1793 building, the oldest Russian structure still standing in Alaska, was originally a storehouse and commissary at Baranov's settlement in Kodiak. —Photo by Frank Whaley, Wien Collection, Anchorage Museum, AMRC-B85-27-1365

arrived to find the settlement struggling. An earthquake in 1788 had flooded the low-lying community and destroyed many of the buildings. The location of the settlement was not ideal anyway—there was little solid, flat ground to build on as well as a lack of timber to build with, so Baranov decided to move the colony about fifty miles north to Pavlovsk (St. Paul) Harbor in 1791. This settlement, called St. Paul, later became the city of Kodiak. Baranov proved to be a good manager, expanding the schools in St. Paul and establishing a shipworks at Resurrection Bay, planting the seed for today's city of Seward.

In 1793 the Shelikhov family welcomed another daughter, called Natalia like her mother. The following year, Natalia and Grigorii's sixth daughter, Elisaveta, was born. That same year, Natalia's request for priests to go to Kodiak Island was finally approved. To help make the arrangements for the clergymen's journey, a Russian noble named Nikolai Rezanov was sent to Irkutz. Educated and handsome, Rezanov, a prominent government official, was well paid and had influence in the court. He was a welcome guest in the Shelikhov home, where he was captured by the charms of the eldest Shelikhov daughter, the pretty and talented Anna. Anna was fourteen, a marriageable age, and Natalia and Grigorii were thrilled when she and Rezanov became engaged. They were married early in 1795.

But once more, the family's happiness was short-lived. In July 1795, Grigorii came down with a high fever. Knowing his illness was grave, Grigorii wrote to Catherine the Great, asking the empress to honor his final wishes. "My wife . . . deserves my full confidence. She with my children and no one else should have possession of my property," he wrote. A short time later, on July 20, 1795, Grigorii Shelikhov died at age forty-eight. Eight days after his death, ten-month-old Elisaveta also passed away, possibly from the same illness. Somehow Natalia, who was pregnant at the time of her husband's death, found the strength to survive these devastating events. Their last child, Grigorii, was born five months after the death of his father, for whom he was named.

As Natalia tried to assume control of the company she had inherited in accordance with Grigorii's wishes, competing trading companies began what has been called "a noisy war" against her, trying to discredit her and disrupt the company with complaints and lawsuits. There was also a dispute with Grigorii's former partner, Ivan Golikov, and his family over the distribution of shares. Further complications ensued when Empress Catherine, whom Natalia hoped would provide her with support, died in November 1796. Catherine was succeeded by her son, Emperor Paul I.

Natalia struggled for the next several years to keep the company going. Luckily she received considerable help from her son-in-law Nikolai Rezanov and from respected local merchant Mikhail Buldakov, who also became her son-in-law. Buldakov, who was probably a business associate and family friend, married Natalia's daughter Avdotia, the "American girl," in early 1798. The bride was fourteen and the groom was thirty.

The following year, the Shelikhov company was reorganized as the Russian-American Company, with both Rezanov and Buldakov as Natalia's partners. Emperor Paul granted the newly formed company exclusive hunting and trading rights on the North American coast above the 55th parallel north (most of present-day Alaska and northern Canada), as well as the Aleutian Islands. The Shelikhovs' dream of a monopoly in Alaska was finally realized.

When the new company was formed, the manager at Kodiak, Aleksander Baranov, built a settlement in a location now called Old Sitka. Three years later, the native Tlingits attacked and destroyed the village. Undeterred, Baranov relocated a few miles south and built the settlement of New Archangel, now the city of Sitka.

When the Russian-American Company was established in 1799, the emperor ordered the company to move its headquarters from

Irkutsk to St. Petersburg, so Natalia planned to make her home there. But before she was able to leave town, little Grigorii died, and Natalia herself was very ill. She remained in Irkutsk until the spring of 1802. By the time she left for St Petersburg, turning over most of the company's business matters to her son-in-law Mikhail Buldakov, she was unwell and weary from grief.

The last few years of Natalia's life were unhappy. In October 1802 her daughter Anna died a few days after giving birth to her second child. Later, discord within the family erupted, apparently over money, and Natalia became estranged from her two sons-in-law, her daughter Avdotia, and perhaps other family members as well. By 1808 her health had worsened. Finally, on March 25, 1810, Natalia Shelikhova died in Moscow at age forty-eight or forty-nine. The details of her death—how she died, why she was in Moscow—are unknown.

Today Natalia is recognized for the importance of her accomplishments. She bravely traveled thousands of miles over frigid ocean waters and difficult and dangerous terrain, often while pregnant. While in Three Saints Bay, she formed good relationships with the Native Alaskans and made great progress in educating Native children and adults. Perhaps most impressively, she successfully ran, nearly by herself, a multimillion-dollar business for almost twenty years. Her management of the Russian American Company's monopoly made her, in fact though not formally, the first woman governor of Russian Alaska. It is little wonder that in 2009 Natalia Shelikhova was one of the first fifty women named to the Alaska Women's Hall of Fame.

Several geographical sites bear the Shelikhov name, among them the strait between Kodiak Island and the Alaska Peninsula and a gulf between Kamchatka and the Siberian mainland. The Three Saints Bay site, where the first settlement stood, was declared a National Historic Landmark in 1978.

MARY ANTISARLOOK

Reindeer Queen

"Reindeer Queen" was only one of many names that identified this half-Russian, half–Inupiaq Eskimo woman who became one of the wealthiest businesswomen in Alaska. At her birth, she was given a Russian name, Palasha (sometimes spelled Palagai) Makrikoff, and an Inupiaq name, Changunak, but she became best known as Mary. Early in life, she was nicknamed "Russian Mary," but later she was called "Sinrock Mary," the "Reindeer Queen," or simply "Reindeer Mary." Some even referred to her as "Queen Mary" and joked about her being royalty. Her two marriages added two more surnames, Antisarlook and Andrewuk, to her moniker over the course of her life.

Mary acquired her reindeer-related nicknames as an adult, after she had earned a fortune raising reindeer on the Seward Peninsula. She and her first husband originally based their herd in the Eskimo village of Sinrock (also spelled Synrock; now spelled Sinuk), located along the Sinuk (formerly spelled Sinrock) River, west of today's Nome. After her husband's death, "Sinrock Mary" moved the animals about 250 miles southeast to Unalakleet, where she spent the remainder of her life.

Mary was still a child when Russia sold Alaska to the United States in 1867, making it a U.S. territory. The area was managed as the Department of Alaska until 1884, when it became the District of Alaska, and it was reorganized as the Territory of Alaska in 1912 (it would not become a state until the mid-twentieth century). Among the many changes brought by the transition was an influx of American administrators, soldiers and sailors, missionaries, traders, whalers, miners, and even settlers. With the Americans came new technologies and divergent cultural attitudes and practices. Mary's unique set of skills made her better suited than most Eskimo women to adapt to these changes.

Mary was born at Redoubt St. Michael, a trading post on the coast of Norton Sound in western Alaska. The exact date of her birth is uncertain, but it is believed to have been in the early 1860s. Redoubt St. Michael—the farthest north of the Russian redoubts, or trading posts—was built by the Russian-American Company in 1833, at a site where the water was deep enough for the company's trading ships to anchor and load. Nearby were villages of Inupiaq Eskimos. The small contingent of Russian traders who manned the redoubt exchanged their European goods for the Inupiaqs' fish, game meat, wild bird eggs, berries, and clothing. Many of these Russians, including Mary's father, married Native women from area villages and had families.

We know that Mary's father was a Russian trader with the surname Makrikoff and her mother was an Inupiaq from a village in the St. Michael area, but their first names are unknown. From childhood, Mary was known for her beautiful dark curly hair—curls probably inherited from her father, since Eskimos typically had straight locks. She grew up bilingual, speaking both Russian and Inupiaq; later she also learned English. Her skills as a translator would prove invaluable in her business.

Although she knew the Russian language and culture, Mary was raised in the Inupiaq tradition. Both girls and boys helped with household chores such as chopping wood, carrying supplies, fetching water, picking berries, butchering meat, cleaning up, and looking after younger children. Girls also learned to weave nets of deer sinew and sew clothes from the skins of various animals. By the time they were adults, most female Inupiaqs were skilled at making winter parkas from deerskin, sable, and muskrat with hoods, hems, and cuffs bordered with wolf fur. Most of the food preparation was also done by women. If they had the time and the inclination, women sometimes hunted small game as well, though men did most of the big-game hunting.

The main big-game animal in northwestern Alaska was the caribou, a large, migratory mammal of the deer family somewhat similar to elk. Eskimos also hunted sea animals such as whales, walruses, and seals. They often traded skins and other items made from these animals with other Native Alaskans and later with Russians and, later still, Americans. The Inupiaq were particularly skilled traders. One Russian naval officer described them as "shrewd, enterprising, sound of judgment, vigilant, gifted with a fine memory, and hospitable." After the arrival of Americans, the Inupiaq quickly learned the English words they needed to trade with them.

Much of this trading was done at the summer trade fairs. The fair at Port Clarence, on the western coast of the Seward Peninsula, usually took place in early July, and later in the summer another fair took place farther east at Kotzebue. There were also a number of smaller fairs throughout the region during the summer months.

In seal-skin boats, natives from miles around paddled to the fair sites, taking such items as cured skins—those of ringed or bearded seals were in high demand—to trade with other groups. The Inupiaqs originally traded with the Yu'piks of St. Lawrence Island as well as the Chukchis of Siberia. By the late 1800s, trading boats from America, Russia, Scandinavia, and elsewhere made a regular round of these fairs, carrying European items, such as tobacco and guns, from one to the next. In addition to trading, fair participants enjoyed feasting, playing games, dancing to the beat of drums, and singing songs, including some Russian tunes they had adopted.

Mary undoubtedly attended some of these fairs, and it was perhaps at one of them that she met Charlie Antisarlook, a full-blooded Inupiaq from Cape Nome, across Norton Sound from St. Michael. By then Mary, in her early twenties, had a tattooed stripe from her lower lip to her chin, which meant "I'm a mature woman." Many Eskimo women were heavily tattooed. They often added more chin stripes to represent their marital status, the number of children they had, and significant life experiences. The tattooing was done using ivory or bone needles and sinew thread dipped in pigment.

Mary and Charlie were married in 1889 and moved to Cape Nome. In the summer of 1890 they went together to the Port Clarence fair, where the newlyweds unexpectly received a job offer. That summer the *Bear*, a sailing vessel serving the American Revenue Cutter Service—a forerunner of today's Coast Guard—had just arrived at Port Clarence. The *Bear's* captain, Michael Healy—known as "Hell-Roaring Mike"—had a number of duties, including arresting seal poachers; carrying mail, supplies, and occasionally passengers; and rescuing stranded sailors. On this voyage, he had been assigned a special task—to conduct a census to find out how many people actually lived in that icebox of a territory the nation had recently acquired. For this, Healy needed interpreters. He hired Mary and Charlie, with whom he developed a good working relationship.

Meanwhile, another passenger on the *Bear*, Dr. Sheldon Jackson, the territory's General Agent for Education, had come to the region to look for suitable sites on which to build schools for Native children. As he explored the Inupiaq settlements in the area, Jackson

Mary Antisarlook, date unknown —Courtesy Jodi Newell

was shocked by what he thought was widespread starvation, which he blamed on the reduced supply of whales and wild caribou—mainstays of the Eskimo diet—caused by European overhunting. Yet the Inupiaq themselves did not seem worried. They were used to periods of scarcity and knew how to survive on fish, seals, and small game, which were still plentiful. Nevertheless, Captain Healy shared Jackson's concerns and encouraged him to act on them.

On his travels to Siberia's Chukchi Peninsula, Jackson observed the Siberians raising herds of domesticated reindeer. Still concerned about poverty among the Eskimos, he developed the idea of importing reindeer from Siberia for the Alaskans to raise. Reindeer could not only help replace the diminishing caribou, he believed, they could also be trained to pull sleds up and down the nearly roadless Alaskan coast. Moreover, encouraging Native Alaskans to become herders rather than hunters would ultimately help them adapt to the European-American culture that was rapidly gaining influence in Alaska.

Unlike caribou, reindeer are not native to Alaska, although the two animals are of the same species. Caribou roamed in wild herds, while their Siberian-European cousins were domesticated like cattle and horses. Due to their natural similarities to caribou, reindeer would be, it seemed, well-suited to the tundra of northwestern Alaska. Herds could roam over its unfenced public lands, grazing year-round on moss, lichens, grasses, and shrubs. In winter, their powerful sense of smell could root out snow-covered moss, which they could dig out with their broad hooves. The size and shape of their hooves also allowed the animal to walk over crusted snow or swampy ground, and the hollow hairs of their coats provided insulation against the cold and gave the animals a natural buoyancy in water.

When Jackson returned to the States, he requested funding for a reindeer-importation project from the U.S. government. In an early report to Congress he said, "to establish schools would be of little service" among what he viewed as starving people. He was convinced that introducing reindeer should be the first step in fulfilling the Natives' basic needs and stablizing their economy. Education would have to wait.

Although Congress did not directly finance Jackson's project, it allowed him to use funds from the Bureau of Education to buy reindeer and to permit the *Bear* to transport the herd. In 1891 Jackson bought sixteen reindeer in Siberia and had them shipped to the Aleutian Islands. He left them there to fend for themselves, and according to historian Dorothy Jean Ray, without someone to care for them, the animals all died.

Jackson himself, however, deemed the experiment a success and bought 171 more reindeer, moving them to Teller Station, an experimental reindeer station at Port Clarence. This time Jackson hired four experienced reindeer herders from the Chukchi Peninsula to accompany the animals. At Teller Station, an apprenticeship program had been established to train Native Alaskans as herders. The program required interested Eskimo men to work under the Chukchi herders for two years (later extended to five years) before being given ownership of their own herds. In addition to free room and board, the apprentices would be paid in reindeer, eventually collecting enough animals to start herds of their own when the time came. Charlie Antisarlook, who had been working as an interpreter and assistant on the *Bear,* was one of the first men to be hired as an apprentice at Teller, in 1892.

At first, few Natives signed up for the program. Most Inupiaq preferred to maintain their traditional way of life—hunting and fishing—rather than learn to raise domestic animals, and many resented the Chukchi outsiders. But Charlie and Mary were willing to give it a try.

The first year did not go well for the Antisarlooks. The superintendent at Teller, Miner Bruce, fired Charlie apparently because he disliked Mary, claiming that she knew "just enough English to make mischief." But Sheldon Jackson, displeased, fired Bruce and hired a new manager, William Thomas (Tom) Lopp, who reinstated both Charlie and Mary. While Charlie worked with the herd, Mary provided household help for Tom Lopp and his wife Ellen, who lived at the station with their children. In 1894 she even helped deliver Ellen's baby.

Alaska reindeer herd, early 1910s —John Zug Album, UAF-1980-68-239, Archives, University of Alaska Fairbanks

Lopp, writing his yearly report for Jackson to present to Congress, summarized the success of the herding program and predicted that "Alaskan herders would become rich and independent men of as much wealth and influence as walrus or whale hunters." This wasn't what Jackson had expected, however. His plan had been to provide food and clothing "for famished and freezing Eskimos," not to make a lucky few Native Alaskans wealthy. Yet Lopp's report inspired Jackson to think bigger. Reindeer herding could potentially give Alaska a whole new economic boost, bringing wealth to the Natives as well as their investors. He continued the program with plans to expand it further.

Interestingly, Lopp described in his report not only the progress of the herding program, but also social life at Teller Station. He told how the Natives had built a new dance hall, where they "feasted and danced half of November and all of December." He continued,

"We gave our herders a taffy pulling on Thanksgiving night and tried to entertain them with a Christmas tree and a Santa Claus on Christmas [Eve]." Apparently the Inupiaq did not know what to make of the strange rituals. "If they were surprised, delighted or gladdened, their faces did not reveal it," Lopp wrote. Christmas Day brought a more successful celebration. "Fourteen sleds arrived from Cape Prince of Wales bringing walrus meat, whale blubber, deerskins, wolverine and wolf skins as presents to the hosts." Lopp gave a "grand masked dance" in the visitors' honor and presented them with "red fox, beaver, otter and other pelts."

After the first year, the Chukchi herders—unpopular among the Natives and American administrators alike—were replaced with reindeer herders from Lapland, an arctic region in Scandinavia. The Lapps arrived at Teller Station in the summer of 1894.

In January 1895, Charlie became the first of the apprentices to receive his own herd. He was chosen because he was considered the most mature Eskimo, eager to work and cooperate, and he could speak English. The U.S. government gave him one hundred reindeer on loan; after five years he would have to give back that number but could keep the increase. After choosing the deer they wanted from the station's herd, Charlie and Mary took their animals about forty-five miles south and set up a ranch in Sinrock, a small Eskimo village on the Sinrock River. There they made their home. Although Charlie and Mary had no children of their own, they adopted a number of Eskimo children who had lost their parents or whose parents couldn't care for them.

Since one of the requirements for Native ownership of reindeer was that the owners had to take on apprentices of their own, relatives and friends of the Antisarlooks also moved to Sinrock to work for Charlie. When the Antisarlooks' adopted children got older, some of them also became herder apprentices. Under Charlie and Mary's tender care, the Sinrock reindeer thrived, and so did the village. As the herd increased in size, more apprentice herders arrived in Sinrock, often with their families, and within a few years it became a sizeable village. "Sinrock Charlie" was on his way to becoming the "Reindeer King" of Alaska.

In the meantime, not long after Charlie and Mary settled in Sinrock, a major event took place in Alaska—gold was discovered in Canada's Yukon Territory in 1896. Within a year, that area—1,000 miles east of Sinrock—was overrun with prospectors. Hearing reports that the Yukon miners were in danger of starving, Sheldon Jackson decided to appropriate some reindeer from his program to feed them. In the fall of 1897 Jackson's men approached Charlie, whose herd had reached 233 deer by then, and told him he had to repay his loan early. Charlie reluctantly relinquished one hundred deer, which cut his herd nearly in half.

But this was not the end of Charlie's and Mary's troubles. Only a few weeks later, eight whaling ships became trapped in ice off Point Barrow, and the crews were running out of food. When word of the disaster reached Washington D.C., an overland relief expedition was organized to aid them. Lt. David Jarvis, a friend of the Antisarlooks, was sent to Sinrock to ask the couple for the rest of their herd. Later, Jarvis wrote how difficult it was to bring himself to ask Charlie and Mary for their deer. "They were old friends," he said. "The deer were his absolute property. . . . He and the people gathered about him were dependent upon the herd for food and clothing."

At first, Mary was resistant, telling Jarvis:

> We are sorry for the people at Point Barrow and we want to help them, but we hate to see our deer go because we are poor and our people in the village are poor and in winter when we cannot get seals we kill a deer and this helps us through the hard times. If we let our deer go, what are we to do? Antisarlook and I have not enough without them to live upon.

Charlie and Mary, Jarvis reported, "held a long and serious con-
sultation." After much anguish, the Antisarlooks struck a deal with
Jarvis. Charlie agreed to accompany Jarvis to Point Barrow with the
herd if Jarvis would make sure the deer were later replaced. In addition, Jarvis made arrangements for Mary and the villagers to receive
provisions from Teller Station at Port Clarence, forty-five miles north
of Sinrock, and from a trading post at Golovnin Bay, about ninety
miles southeast. In January 1898 Charlie and his reindeer set off
with Jarvis, along with Tom Lopp and the Port Clarence herd, on the
seven-hundred-mile journey to Point Barrow in bitterly cold weather.

When, after weeks traveling over icy terrain in below-zero temperatures, the relief expedition finally reached the whalers at Barrow,
they were amazed to discover that no one was starving. The Inupiaq Eskimos in Barrow had provided the whalers with caribou,
fish, and wild fowl. Still, Jarvis and his party had little choice but
to leave the reindeer there anyway. Only some of them were later
killed for food, and the rest were turned over to the government.

Meanwhile, back at Sinrock, the situation was not good. Over the
winter, Mary had had trouble getting the promised supplies, which
the village desperately needed—the seal hunt had been only par-
tially successful and the fishing season did not begin until summer.
Somehow the village survived until the *Bear* arrived with supplies
in early summer, while Charlie was still in Barrow. The *Bear's* captain—now Francis Tuttle—gave Mary enough provisions to last
until Charlie returned in late summer 1898. But it was another year
and a half before the Antisarlooks would receive their replacement
reindeer from the government.

Around the same time Charlie got home from Barrow, in September 1898, three Swedish immigrants found gold in Anvil Creek,
a stream near Cape Nome (Charlie's hometown), about twenty-five
miles east of Sinrock. The "Lucky Swedes," as the prospectors were
nicknamed, formed the Cape Nome Mining District and staked

claims for themselves and their relatives. Later a soldier from the U.S. Army post that had been established at St. Michael found gold near the mouth of Cape Nome's Snake River. By the following summer, a new gold rush had begun in northwestern Alaska, this one practically in the Antisarlooks' backyard.

Thousands of fortune seekers descended on the beaches of Cape Nome, where the "Lucky Swedes" founded a mining town called Nome. At the height of the Nome gold rush, hundreds of tents lined the beaches for miles, extending to the area where Mary and Charlie's reindeer grazed. The Antisarlooks and other Eskimos in the region had to turn their energies to protecting their homes, pastures, and hunting grounds. But there was no way for them to protect themselves from what came next. Accompanying the newcomers were diseases—especially measles and influenza—to which Native Alaskans had no immunities. By the end of 1900, the Seward Peninsula would lose more than half its Native population, mostly from the flu and measles.

In a news story about the crisis, Washington, D.C.'s *Evening Times* printed a letter from Sheldon Jackson to the *Bear*'s captain Francis Tuttle, written on August 1, 1900, in which he described the devastation:

> I have just returned from a visit to the Government reindeer station [at Port Clarence] . . . and find the influenza, which is epidemic along the whole coastline among the Eskimo, is raging with great violence. . . . The Rev. Mr. Brevig . . . reports that fully half of the Eskimo around the station have died. . . . In some cases whole families have disappeared, both parents and children being dead. In others the parents and some of the children have died, leaving young children orphans, with no near relatives to feed or care for them.
>
> . . . [T]here are not sufficient numbers of well people to catch [salmon] and thus provide food both for the present and for next winter. . . .

> ... The Rev. Mr. Brevig, although not a physician, has set up a
> few tents and is running a temporary hospital as best he can. . . .
> He is in great need of pilot bread, flour, and clothing . . . .

That same summer, the Native residents of Sinrock suffered a serious epidemic of measles. Among the dead there were Charlie Antisarlook and one of his brothers, Achickchick. Charlie had contracted the measles on July 15, 1900, and he died two weeks later. His death made headlines in the *Nome Daily News* on August 2, 1900: "Reindeer King Dead. Charlie Antisarlook, Richest Eskimo of Northern Alaska." Mary was now a widow.

At the time of his death, Sinrock Charlie's wealth included about four hundred reindeer as well as mining claims. During the epidemic, many of the herders had been too sick to care for the reindeer, so a good number of them wandered off or were stolen, leaving around 360 by the end of the year. Charlie's relatives and apprentices had claims on some of the herd, so the reindeer were distributed among them. Mary inherited her share under American inheritance laws, though in Eskimo tradition, women were not allowed to own property, so the entire herd would have been awarded to his brothers. The official decree gave most of them, 272, to Mary, while Achickchick's wife and teenage son received ownership of 45 and 10, respectively; the two surviving brothers—Koktoak (also spelled Kotak or Kuktiak), age twenty-one, and Angolook (or Ongalook), age sixteen, took 12 and 9 deer, respectively. In addition, two of Charlie's apprentices received 6 each.

Later, Kotoak and Angolook filed complaints with the Bureau of Education stating that under Eskimo law they, not Mary, should have inherited Charlie's herd. Tom Lopp, who had recently replaced Sheldon Jackson as bureau chairman, explained to them that United States law was in effect, giving major ownership of the deer to Mary and her adopted children. However, he suggested to

Mary that she give the brothers two female deer each to soothe any hard feelings within the family.

With Charlie's death, it was now up to Mary to take over the herd's management in Sinrock. Having worked alongside Charlie for the past eight years, she knew how to take care of the deer, and there was a ready market for their meat and their hides in nearby Nome. But Nome had become chaotic. Gold miners roamed the streets, drinking and fighting and causing other problems associated with overcrowded mining camps, such as diseases spread by contaminated water and unsanitary living conditions. The miners were also stealing and killing reindeer. They set fires and shot rifles at Mary's herd to try to frighten the deer into scattering so that they might capture a few. Some miners offered Mary money or liquor for her deer, and a few reportedly even proposed marriage in an effort to share in her wealth. But she stood firm.

Mary, described as "tall and powerful" and "a large imposing figure," was not intimidated by roughneck miners. A photograph shows the "Reindeer Queen" with a broad, determined smile, her curly hair escaping around the edges of a scarf. But Sheldon Jackson and Tom Lopp feared that Mary would lose her reindeer and advised her to relocate from Nome to the Eaton Reindeer Station at Unalakleet, on the Unalakleet (sometimes spelled Unalaklik) River, close to her own hometown of St. Michael. Fort St. Michael, they pointed out, would provide her with plenty of customers.

Mary decided to move to Unalakleet in December 1901. Charlie's relatives would also go there with their reindeer. But Mary had trouble finding someone to take charge of moving the herd until J. T. Lindseth, an American who used to work for Charlie, offered to help. As soon as he took the herd, however, Lindseth, a man Mary thought she could trust, attempted to get power of attorney to take control of Mary's reindeer and sell them, claiming that Mary had put him in charge and he was handling the business. When Mary heard about it, she immediately put a stop to Lindseth's legal maneuvering.

Yet Lindseth was not finished trying to swindle Mary. Upon arriving in Unalakleet with the reindeer in February 1902, he claimed that she owed him a salary for driving the herd from Nome. She replied that she had not hired him, he had volunteered. Nevertheless, she offered him three prime deer, worth about $150 each, as payment for his trouble. Lindseth demanded more. Mary refused, whereupon he filed suit against her, asking for $553.45. The case was heard two years later in the district court in Nome. It attracted considerable attention because it was unusual for an Eskimo, particularly a woman, to be a defendant in a civil suit. In the end, the jurors ruled in Mary's favor.

Not long after moving to Unalakleet, Mary married an Inupiaq man, Andrew Andrewuk. Andrew had no interest in herding reindeer and left running the business entirely to Mary. Her herd eventually grew to 1,500 deer, the largest herd of any individual owner. Just as "Sinrock Charlie" had been called the wealthiest man in Alaska, now "Sinrock Mary" was considered the wealthiest woman. She did not personally care for the reindeer—she paid workers at Eaton Station to do that—but she kept close track of the herd.

While Mary was known to be strong-willed and hardheaded in her business affairs, she was also known for her generosity. In addition to the children she and Charlie had adopted in Sinrock, she took in more children in Unalakleet and used much of her wealth to care for needy Eskimos in the community.

After 1907 the government began a program to transfer more reindeer from European and American owners to Native Alaskans. While this brought more wealth into Native communities, the program also disrupted the Eskimos' traditional way of life. They were used to sharing everything with their neighbors, and the idea of individual ownership was strange to them. As disagreements flared up, the Natives had no clear way to deal with them. In the meantime, gold mining in Alaska was dwindling, and as the miners left, so did the market for reindeer products.

To help ease the problems, the Bureau of Education came up with the idea of holding regular Reindeer Fairs on Alaska's Seward Peninsula to celebrate the Native reindeer herders and encourage more cooperation among them. The weeklong event would feature games, competitions, food, music, parades, and lots of conversation. The first fair, held in 1915, was a great success, as were the next two. But in 1918, another deadly flu epidemic struck Alaska, and the fair was cancelled. The devastation brought on by the epidemic created chaos in the reindeer industry, and the Bureau stopped sponsoring the fairs.

By the end of the epidemic in 1919, some villages had lost 85 percent of their population. With the deaths of so many herders, deer were left unattended, and many wandered off to join herds of wild

Native herders posed with deer at Reindeer Fair, 1915? —Lomen Brothers photo, John Urban Collection, Anchorage Museum, AMRC-B64-1-436

caribou. The remaining reindeer became so mixed together that the herders could not tell which deer belonged to which owner. In the meantime, the animals continued to multiply, and by the 1920s, the reindeer population was outgrowing its grazing ranges. As one official put it in 1926, "Alaska's food, the reindeer, is eating up Alaska."

In addition to these stresses, a white American industrialist, Carl Lomen, had invested heavily in Alaska reindeer beginning in 1914 and competed (some believed unfairly) with the Native herders for the relatively small reindeer market. It was discouraging for the Eskimos to see their herds grow in numbers while their value decreased.

In 1929 the U.S. government transferred responsibility for the reindeer program from the federal Bureau of Education to the Alaska territorial governor, George A. Parks. The federal government did not pull out completely, however; the same year, a federal Reindeer Committee was organized to look into the herders' continuing problems. Then, in October 1929, the stock market crashed, sending the United States into the Great Depression. Carl Lomen soon went broke and abandoned his reindeer business, but the Native herders were still struggling.

Further committees were organized into the 1930s until Congress passed the Alaska Reorganization Act of 1936, an attempt to help Native Alaskans govern themselves. The following year, the Reindeer Act was passed, giving Alaska Natives the exclusive right to engage in the reindeer trade in the territory. It also transferred control of the reindeer program back to the federal government, placing it under the authority of the U.S. Office of Indian Affairs.

While these developments might have helped Native herders, the changes came, as it turned out, too late. Over the next several years, the reindeer of Alaska, previously so abundant, began to die out at a rapid pace. It is not known for certain what caused the die-off, but it was likely a combination of factors. For one thing,

Mary Antisarlook, 1938? —Lomen Family Papers, UAF-1972-71-2279, Archives, University of Alaska Fairbanks

the overpopulation of reindeer of the 1920s destroyed the grazing lands, and many deer starved. Secondly, an increasing number of wolves, attracted by the bounty of deer in the early 1900s, killed a good number of the animals in subsequent years. In addition, significant numbers of reindeer left their domesticated herds and ran off with their wild cousins, the caribou, during the chaos of the 1920s and '30s. The decline continued into the 1950s, by which time Alaska's reindeer industry had become all but extinct.

As for Reindeer Mary, she fared all right. She remained in Unalakleet for the rest of her life, surrounded by her adopted children, their children, and other relatives and friends. Her second husband, Andrew Andrewuk, died in 1931, but Mary lived well into her eighties. Her herd was managed at Eaton Station, but she visited them often, and she loved to sit on the porch of her cabin, telling local children stories about her beloved reindeer. Even after her death in 1948, Mary's legend as the "Reindeer Queen" continued to grow.

Newspapers throughout the nation carried the news of Sinrock Mary's passing. She was remembered not only as a successful business owner, an extraordinary accomplishment for an Eskimo woman in those days, but also as a caring and committed member of her community, a much-loved figure among her own people and in the larger world.

Fifty years after Mary's death, in 2000, filmmaker Maria Brook made a documentary of this remarkable woman's life called *Reindeer Queen: The True Story of Sinrock Mary*. The film opens with a modern Alaskan describing how, while driving his truck near Teller, he spotted a large herd of reindeer through the mist. The locals told him there were no reindeer around—what he saw must have been the "ghost herd" of Sinrock Mary.

By the time Mary died, Alaska's great reindeer era had long been over, but her grandchildren remembered the old days, when people called her "Queen Mary," the wealthiest woman in Alaska.

Anthropologist Dorothy Ray noted in her 1984 article "Sinrock Mary: From Eskimo Wife to Reindeer Queen" that, although she may have been a queen of industry, Mary never lost sight of her Inupiaq roots:

> Mary remained in outlook an Eskimo woman, who fished for salmon and tomcod, dried seal meat and fish for the winter, picked berries and greens, and prepared skins for sewing. Above all, her caring for the more unfortunate endeared her to her fellow Eskimos. . . . She was one of the first Eskimo women to play a role successfully in two cultures, for she combined a commercial success, highly regarded by the white man, with qualities [such as generosity and caring for others] greatly esteemed by the Eskimo.

RUSTY DOW

"A Real Sourdough"

Rusty Dow liked to say she had three loves: her husband, trucks, and painting. The husband was Russell Dow, who had worked as a photographer, a miner, a ski instructor, a builder, and an engineer. The trucks were what Rusty was best known for, having started several of her own trucking businesses and having been the first woman to drive the 1,700-mile Alaska-Canadian ("Alcan") Highway during World War II. And painting, a passion Rusty rediscovered later in life, revealed the softer side of a woman who described herself as "all muscle."

Driving a truck was something Rusty had been doing since long before she moved to Alaska in 1934. Born Benzie Ola Scott on June 15, 1894, in Wallis Station, Texas, to farm workers John (Jack) and Ward Scott, she grew up on farms and ranches and learned to drive a full-size truck when she was very young. The eldest of the Scotts' four children, Benzie was the only girl, but she easily kept up with her brothers Homer, Zoell, and John Jr. Her masses of curly red hair earned her the nickname "Rusty" at a young age, and she went by that name for the rest of her life.

The Scott family moved often, following work opportunities throughout the American Southwest, often living in a tent. The children all pitched in, taking whatever work was available—picking crops, hauling loads, making repairs, and doing other odd jobs. Not long after Rusty graduated from high school in Carlsbad, New Mexico, at age sixteen, the Scotts moved to the rapidly growing city of Los Angeles, California, where Rusty used the family's two-ton Chevy pickup to transport local farmers' produce to market. The family got by all right in California, but with the onset of the Great Depression in 1929, they, like other Americans, started thinking about new opportunities.

That opportunity turned out to be Alaska. Homesteads in the territory had been available since 1898, but few Americans cared to try to farm in such a harsh and isolated place. During the Depression, however, a number of hardy souls decided to take the risk. One of these was Rusty's younger brother Zoell, who signed up for a homestead near Palmer, in Alaska's Matanuska Valley, and moved there. Not long afterward, Zoell invited his family to join him way up north. The adventurous Rusty did not hesitate. In 1934 Rusty, age forty, and her parents set off for the Last Frontier, taking the faithful Chevy truck with them. They traveled by ship to Seward and then by train to Palmer.

At the time, the Matanuska Valley was little settled, although coal and gold mines had been operating on the valley's rim for years, and by 1916 the Alaska Railroad was running through the valley, extending from Seward, about 150 miles south of Palmer, to Fairbanks, about three hundred miles north. In addition, a new development, which Zoell had no doubt heard about, was soon to get under way there. President Franklin Roosevelt had introduced a plan—officially signed into law in January 1935—offering free homesteads in the Matanuska-Susitna Valley (Mat-Su Valley for short) to impoverished farm families in the upper Midwest. It was hoped that the Matanuska Colony, as the project was called, would grow the population and create new economic opportunties not only for the colonists themselves but also for the other residents of the valley.

When Rusty and her parents arrived in Palmer, the few roads in the area were crude and rough. Heading north into the Talkeetna Mountains, a bulldozed dirt road led seventeen miles from Palmer to the Independence gold mine at Hatcher Pass. Rusty immediately

Rusty Scott and her truck, Palmer, Alaska, 1939 —Russ Dow Papers, Archives and Special Collections, Consortium Library, University of Alaska Anchorage

recognized that the mine presented a niche that she and her truck could fill. She started a trucking service that hauled freight and supplies to the mine and provided rides into Palmer for the miners. After a while, noticing that the miners often carried bundles of dirty clothes into town, she leased a laundry operation in Palmer and ran it as a side business.

Rusty's trucking service was very popular, as was Rusty herself. Cheerful and friendly, she entertained her passengers as she drove. In town, she took part in many local activities, and at community dances she never lacked partners. It didn't hurt that she was one of about three single women in Palmer.

Two years after arriving in Alaska, when the road between Palmer and Anchorage was completed, Rusty bought a second-hand sedan, which could carry more passengers than her truck, and used it to shuttle miners back and forth to Anchorage, where they liked to spend their nights off drinking and carousing. In the wee hours of the morning, she would round up the drunken miners, drive them back to the mining camp, and "deliver them safe and sound to the bunkhouse." One of the men she "delivered" was Russell Dow.

New Hampshire native Russ Dow, an expert skier, first arrived in Alaska as a Dartmouth student taking part in a university-sponsored geological expedition of the Mount Crillon area in 1934. Later he studied engineering and photography at Harvard. In 1937 he returned to Alaska, where he worked odd jobs and took pictures in the Mat-Su Valley. The following year, he took a job at the Hatcher Pass mine. One February evening in 1939, he got a ride home from Anchorage from a feisty redhead he had heard about and seen before but never met—the famous Rusty Scott. As they chatted on the way back to the mining camp, Russ discovered he was smitten.

After that, on his days off, Russ started skiing the seventeen miles to Palmer to see Rusty at the laundry. Although she had no interest in marriage, Rusty soon warmed up to this intelligent but rugged young man. They shared many interests and both were always ready to try something new. When he proposed, she accepted. Rusty never told Russ her real age—she was in fact twenty-one years older than her fiancé. They were married on New Year's Eve of 1939, only ten months after they met. After the wedding, the couple moved to Anchorage, occupying a log cabin on Bootleggers Cove.

Naturally, Russ soon became involved with the Anchorage Ski Club, which had been established in 1937. The club managed the City Ski Bowl slope, located on the bluff overlooking Ship Creek, very close to the Dows' cabin. The slope had been used as early as 1917, but in 1939 the Civilian Conservation Corps built the territory's first rope tow, promoted as "a modern ski aid," and a thirty-meter ski jump at City Ski. By 1940 skiing had become the most popular winter sport in Alaska. Rusty enjoyed the sport, too, as shown in a photograph of her on the slopes with Russ. It was probably Russ who taught Rusty how to ski.

Anchorage in 1940 had a population of about 3,000, but it was growing rapidly. Although the United States had not yet entered World War II, the war raging in Europe and Asia put the U.S. armed forces on alert. Should American soil be attacked, the military wanted to be ready. The coastline of western Alaska was a strategic (and therefore vulnerable) location along the northern transportation routes of the Pacific Ocean. By 1940 the government had begun a massive military buildup in Anchorage, constructing Fort Richardson and Elmendorf Air Base and bringing in thousands of soldiers and civilian workers to staff the posts. Before long, Anchorage's Merrill Field became one of the busiest airports in the nation.

Upon moving to Anchorage, Russ took a job as a bulldozer operator at Fort Richardson while Rusty continued her trucking service to Palmer and the Independence Mine. Later that year, Russ was hired to teach the soldiers skiing, which was part of their training in

Russ and Rusty at City Ski Bowl, probably early 1940s —Russ Dow Papers,
Archives and Special Collections, Consortium Library, University of Alaska Anchorage

Alaska. In 1941 Russ and the Anchorage Ski Club helped the army establish a new ski area, Arctic Valley, overlooking Anchorage in the Chugach Mountains. That same year, Rusty took a job as an officer's driver at the fort. By that time, the United States was supplying the Allies with weapons and heavy equipment, and the war in Europe and Asia was looming closer.

On December 7, 1941, the Japanese bombed the U.S. Navy at Pearl Harbor, Hawaii, and President Roosevelt declared war the following day. Russ and Rusty were now part of the civilian war effort under the Alaska Defense Command. Their cabin on Bootleggers Cove had an unobstructed view of Cook Inlet, and the Dows were asked to report any suspicious vessels they saw entering the area.

Since 1940 the army had been worried about the possibility of a Japanese attack on Alaska. With no highway access from Seward to their bases in Anchorage and beyond, the railroad between those two cities was a crucial supply route and thus a likely target. In 1941 the government began work on an alternative line. Should rail service from Seward be disrupted, supplies could be taken to Anchorage from Whittier, which had access to the sea at Prince William Sound and was much closer than Seward.

A major obstacle between Anchorage and Whittier was Maynard Mountain, which was too steep to lay tracks over. The Army Corps of Engineers decided to tunnel through the mountain instead. The tunnel, which would be two and a half miles long and hundreds of feet deep, was drilled from both sides of the mountain at once. The design proved to be so accurate that when the workers reached the center of the tunnel, the two drills broke through only inches apart.

In June 1942, while the Whittier Tunnel was still under construction, the Japanese invaded the western Aleutian Islands. The enemy occupied Attu and Kiska for over a year before American and Canadian forces were able to expel them. In the meantime, the military stepped up the pace on their projects on mainland Alaska, including the tunnel and rail line.

The Whittier Tunnel was finished in November 1943. Before the railroad tracks were laid, a "Holing Through" ceremony was planned to celebrate the tunnel's completion. As part of the festivities, a number of high-ranking army officers and dignitaries were to be driven through the tunnel. Rusty wondered who would be chosen to drive them. She mentioned to a colonel at Fort Richardson that she would love to have the assignment. Her driving skills and plucky attitude were well known in Anchorage—Maj. Gen. Simon Buckner, the commanding general in Alaska, called her "a real sourdough"—and she was given the job. She was the only woman who took part in the ceremony.

By this time, Rusty was a minor celebrity. Newspapers reported on the "girl sourdough" who did a man's job as well as (if not better than) a man. One article described how, when her truck got stuck in snow, she carried freight on her back and walked it in on snowshoes. It was clear she had made herself indispensible around Fort Richardson. Her supervisor on the base was quoted as saying, "I couldn't get along without Rusty," and the Anchorage police chief said she was "twenty-four carat gold."

Rusty's most notable driving assignment was yet to come. Until the war, there were no roads through Canada linking Alaska to the American states. To get to and from the territory, travelers had to take either a ship or a plane. With America's entry into the war, Alaska's transportation systems became susceptible to attack, so the military concluded that an overland route to Alaska was strategically vital. The Army Corps of Engineers planned a road to link Dawson Creek, British Columbia—where it would connect to Canada's existing road system into the United States—with Delta Junction, Alaska—where it could connect to an existing road leading north to Fairbanks, and from there to other towns in Alaska. The Alaska-Canadian Highway project was approved by Congress in February 1942, and work began a month later.

Building the Alcan Highway, as it was usually referred to, was considered the biggest construction project since the Panama Canal, which took America ten years to build. The highway would cross about 1,700 rugged miles of "frozen ground, steep inclines, swampy areas, icy cold streams, and very long distances from the source of supplies."

The ambitious endeavor required a huge workforce—11,000 soldiers (one-third of whom were African American) and 7,500 civilians. Crews were set up at both end points—Dawson Creek and Delta Junction—and in the middle at Whitehorse, Yukon Territory. Living out of shacks and tents and eating mostly army field rations, these workers faced long hours of backbreaking labor, toiling through dust and mud, rocky cliffs and thick vegetation, muggy heat and frigid cold, and unrelenting swarms of mosquitoes. Yet these intrepid crews pushed through all obstacles to complete what was called the "pioneer road" (basically a "rough draft" of the permanent road) in only seven months.

A dedication of the highway was held on November 20, 1942, at a spot called Soldiers Summit, in Yukon Territory, about fifty miles from the Alaska border. The ceremony officially opened the road for military use, though parts of it were not passable until improvements were finished in 1943, and no one had yet driven it the whole way.

In late spring of 1944 the entire highway was deemed driveable, although due to wartime restrictions, permits were required to use it. Rusty longed for the opportunity to drive the history-making road. One day she had casually mentioned to General Buckner that she wanted to drive two famous roadways before she died: the Burma Road in China and the Alcan Highway. The general did not forget the conversation. He could not send her to China, of course, but he could fulfill her second wish. In early June, Rusty received orders to fly to Fairbanks. When she arrived, she was shown an old ten-wheel Studebaker six-by-six and told to familiarize herself with it. She would be taking it, she found out, all the way down the Alcan to Dawson Creek.

On June 4, 1944, the truck was loaded with five tons of concrete, bound for Whitehorse. From there Rusty would take another load to Dawson Creek. As the first woman to attempt to drive the Alcan Highway, Rusty Dow was big news in Alaska, Canada, and the States. Reporters and photographers were there to see her off, and more would be waiting along the route to track her progress. As she took the wheel, the transportation officer told her, "Goodbye, good luck, and keep her rolling."

Rusty and her army truck, 1944 —Russ Dow Papers, Archives and Special Collections, Consortium Library, University of Alaska Anchorage

Keeping her rolling, however, was not easy. Although it was nearly summer and the road was partly paved, it still had plenty of rough spots, and the road-worn Studebaker was temperamental. On her first day of driving, a flat tire slowed Rusty's progress, and she had to rustle up a spare. Three days later she reached Whitehorse and delivered the cement. The Studebaker was replaced with another truck, but that one wasn't much better. The next morning, the second truck was loaded with tractor parts and baggage to be delivered to Dawson Creek, and Rusty was off again.

Outside of Whitehorse, two forest fires were raging, so Rusty had to make her way through miles of thick smoke. Later, the truck's engine quit and she had to replace a broken wire. In wet spots, the road turned to deep mud, and where it was dry, the dust was choking and blinding. Stops were few and far between, and arriving at the stopovers at odd hours sometimes meant missing meals. Rusty had been given army food rations for emergencies, but on the seventh day she opened a package to discover that leaking gasoline had soaked through and ruined all her provisions. She decided to keep driving to the next stop.

Rusty drove through the night, unwittingly passing the next stop because she couldn't see it in the dark. She finally arrived at a town at 2:30 a.m. The town, she realized, was Dawson Creek—she'd made it! Her wish to drive the Alcan had become a reality. Even though it was the middle of the night, army personnel and townspeople at Dawson Creek welcomed her with congratulations and a long-awaited hot meal. By morning, the newspapers were there to get the story and take pictures of the gutsy lady truck driver before she set off for the return trip to Fairbanks with a load of tires.

Rusty arrived back in Fairbanks on June 18. While on the road she had turned fifty, though she did not mention this, as she never revealed her age. Her accomplishment was reported in newspapers throughout North America. Rusty Dow was not only the first woman to drive the Alcan, she was also, as she liked to point out, the first person of either sex to drive it both ways.

After the historic trip, Rusty's life returned to normal. She continued to drive trucks for the military until the war ended in the summer of 1945. After that, with their army jobs over, the Dows were uncertain what they wanted to do or where they wanted to live. They left Alaska for an extended tour of the forty-eight states, but in the end they realized that Alaska was the only place that felt like home. Plenty of homesteads were still available from the government, so Russ and Rusty started looking around the Mat-Su Valley for the perfect spot. They found it on the Knik River, only ten miles south of Palmer. In 1947 the Dows started in on improving their property, clearing the land and cutting twenty-foot logs for a cabin, which the couple built themselves. They were moved in by the end of the summer.

From their new home, Rusty revived her trucking service between Palmer and Anchorage, and Russ began working at a power plant near Eklutna Lake, about thirty miles northwest of Anchorage. Later, Rusty joined Russ at the plant, a job she held from 1950 to 1955. It was during this postwar period that Rusty's youthful love of art became rekindled. In her busy younger days, she had had little time to pursue her interest in painting, but after the war her life slowed down and she began dabbling again. Her favorite subjects were Alaskan landscapes and wildlife, but she also liked to paint portraits of ordinary people, especially truckers and construction workers.

Rusty had never had any formal instruction in art, but she read a lot of books on painting techniques. One of them was *Adventures in Marine Painting* by Stanley Woodward, a well-known Massachusetts artist specializing in seascapes. Rusty wrote to him, and he replied, inviting her to take part in a workshop he was conducting at his art school in Boston. After attending the workshop in the summer of 1949, Rusty returned to Alaska with an intensified passion for painting.

She started experimenting with fluorescent oil paints that glowed under a blacklight. Several of these paintings later won awards and earned her a reputation as an innovative artist. She also designed postcards and Christmas cards, which were very popular. She even taught a few art classes at the local junior college. But Alaska had few venues where artists could display their work, and Rusty saw a chance to do something about that. The annual Mat-Su Valley Fair in Palmer included such activities as a baby show, boxing matches, horse races, and vegetable-growing contests, but no art show. Rusty lobbied the fair's board of directors to add an art contest to the schedule and offered to organize it herself. The board adopted her suggestion, and the art competition proved to be a hit. Rusty joined the fair board and continued managing the art show for the next fifteen years.

In 1956 the fair in Palmer became the official Alaska State Fair (even though Alaska was not actually a state until 1959). The fair of 1960 was very exciting. Not only was it the event's twenty-fifth anniversary, but attendees were also treated to a special visitor—presidential candidate John F. Kennedy. In the speech he made to the enthusiastic fairgoers, Kennedy noted that he was the first presidential candidate to campaign for Alaska's three electoral votes. He praised "the courage and determination which it took to build this valley." No one exemplified this courage and determination better than Rusty Dow.

Over the years, many of Rusty's paintings earned ribbons at various art shows in Alaska, and in the 1970s several of her paintings were permanently installed at the Palmer Public Library. In 1983 her artwork was exhibited in a special showing at the Alaska Historical and Transportation Museum in Palmer. She was also honored by the Alaska legislature, which in 1988 issued a proclamation praising her achievements.

In 1971 the state of Alaska built a retirement complex in Palmer, one of several "Pioneer Homes" established especially for the aging "pioneers" who had lived in Alaska for twenty or more years. Not long after the home was built, Rusty's health began to fail and she moved in. Although she had to give up driving a truck, she cheerfully accepted a wheelchair as a substitute, and her spunky personality never deserted her. She had many friends within and outside the Pioneers' Home, and Russ visited her just about every day. In her wheelchair, Rusty continued to attend the State Fair and other community events in Palmer for many years. Finally, on June 18, 1989, Benzie "Rusty" Scott Dow died in the Mat-Su Valley Hospital in Palmer. She had just turned ninety-five. Russell Dow died only three years later.

The city of Palmer has grown since the Dows lived there. Its current population is nearly 6,000. Thanks to the Matanuska Colony and other farmers in the area, it remains an agricultural community—it is the only town in Alaska that is mainly sustained by farming—but it also offers industry, recreation, and cultural activities. The Independence Mine permanently closed its operations in 1951, but in 1980 it was developed as an Alaska State Historical Park, drawing in tourists to further boost the valley's economy. The park features first-rate recreational facilities and is especially popular for skiing.

Fort Richardson is now a multipurpose facility, used partly for the military—it is the home of the Alaska National Guard—and partly for nonmilitary state operations. The Palmer Pioneers' Home is still there, serving veterans and other seniors in the Mat-Su Valley, and the art exhibit and contest Rusty created at the Alaska State Fair in Palmer continues to be a major attraction every year.

The Whittier Tunnel was renamed the Anton Anderson Memorial Tunnel, for Alaska Railroad chief engineer and Anchorage mayor Anton Anderson, in 1976. In 2000 a paved road was laid between the tracks, making the tunnel accessible to both train and motor traffic. It is the longest dual-purpose tunnel in North America.

The Alcan Highway, now called simply the Alaska Highway, has been improved many times since it was built. Its route has been shortened to less than 1,400 miles, and the entire length is now paved. Travelers who drive it today may not find the obstacles Rusty ran into, but it is still isolated in many places and remains a relatively challenging, though stunningly beautiful, drive. In 1996 the highway was named an International Historical Engineering Landmark, an honor it shares with the Panama Canal and the Eiffel Tower.

Only a few people living in Anchorage and the Mat-Su Valley today knew Rusty personally, but she and Russ are widely remembered for all they did for the war effort and for Alaska. A collection of Rusty's papers and artwork as well as Russ's many photographs has been preserved by the Consortium Library at the University of Alaska Anchorage. These artifacts help keep Rusty's memory alive, as do the many newspaper and magazine articles that were written about her in her lifetime. As the *Milwaukee Journal* put it in 1942, Rusty was "one of those fantastic characters only Alaska can produce."

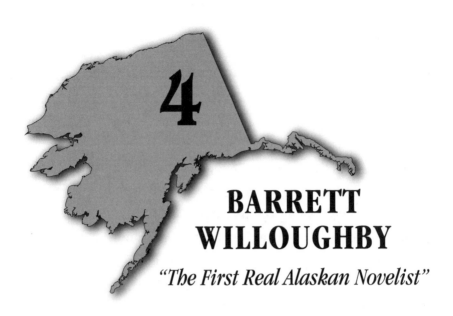

BARRETT WILLOUGHBY

"The First Real Alaskan Novelist"

Barrett Willoughby loved Alaska—the rainforests of the southeast and the tundra of the interior; the wild storms of the Inside Passage, aboard her father's boat; the totem poles of the Tlingit Indian villages; the Northern Lights. She loved Alaska so much, she could not help sharing her feelings. In her books, magazine articles, and interviews, Barrett Willoughby was practically a one-woman tourism bureau for the territory, encouraging those in the States who thought of Alaska as a desolate land of snow and ice to visit the place and experience its unique loveliness for themselves.

In the 1920s, '30s, and '40s, Barrett Willoughby was a bestselling author and minor celebrity. Two of her novels were made into Hollywood movies. But by the late 1950s, her meticulous, evocative descriptions and romantic plots seemed outdated in the literary world, and she had trouble selling her final novel. Today, decades after her death, most of her work is out of print, and the only significant recognition she has received is a biography by the late Nancy Warren Ferrell, poignantly entitled *Barrett Willoughby: Alaska's Forgotten Lady.* Yet she was too colorful a personality and too skilled a writer to be so easily forgotten.

Barrett Willoughby was born Florence Barrett in Berlin, Wisconsin, in May 1886. Her father was Martin Barrett, an incorrigible wanderer whom she described as "a happy-go-lucky Irishman." Her mother was a German immigrant named Florence Klink. The two had met and married in Wisconsin when Martin was thirty-seven and Florence was seventeen. Named after her mother, baby Florence (called Flo or Flossie) was their second child and only daughter. Her brother Lawrence (Loll) was a year or two older, and Frederick (Fred or Freddy) arrived about six years after his sister. By that time, the Barretts had moved to Washington state, probably the Seattle area, where the two older Barrett children would later attend boarding school.

The first home the future writer remembered was a clipper-style schooner, "which my father sailed along the glamorous, uncharted Alaskan shores in search of gold and adventure." News of gold discoveries in the north had captured Martin Barrett's imagination, and sometime after Fred was born in 1892, Martin bought a second-hand schooner named the *Leslie,* which his daughter later referred to as the *Tyee,* and the family sailed for several years along Alaska's southeast coastline. Later, as Barrett Willoughby, Flo wrote that her father "could sail daringly through rock-spiked channels" and roaring storms. As she put it, "Let the black night howl and the black billows fling themselves over the deck! Nothing could happen to us while Dad stood out there at the unhoused wheel."

The children's schoolroom, Barrett recalled, "was the after-deck of a schooner, the teacher my Irish father sitting on the water cask, spinning yarns and pointing out the places of their happening as we sailed along." During their travels, the family often anchored at various trading posts along the coast, where the three young Barretts were sometimes the first white children the local Natives had ever seen. In her writings, Barrett described arriving on Kayak Island during a Tlingit potlatch and watching mesmerized as the dancers whirled to the beat of sealskin drums. While in Kayak, she and her brother Loll caught codfish off the stern of the *Tyee* and sold them for five cents each to a trader she called the "White Chief." She claimed that it was this trader who was responsible for a later episode that nearly cost the Barrett family their lives.

Martin, having heard rumors of placer gold flakes on the shores of the remote and barren Middleton Island, sailed there with the family in September 1896. Upon their arrival, Martin agreed to sell the *Tyee* to the White Chief in exchange for some cash and supplies along with the chief's promise to return for them before winter set in. With this agreement, he left the Barretts on the shore with their food provisions and belongings and sailed away.

Middleton Island, in the Gulf of Alaska some seventy miles away from the mainland, was edged by steep, wave-cut bluffs and reefs that made for dangerous boat landings. Except for rice grass and a few scrubby spruce trees, the island had little vegetation, edible or otherwise. The first day there, the Barretts pitched a tent and stashed their provisions a little bit inland, where they thought the food would be safe from high-tide waters. The family planned to move the next day into a deserted hunter's cabin on the other side of the island. That night, however, the tide came in and seawater swept over their supplies, ruining most of the food.

In the weeks that followed, the Barretts lived on "musty oatmeal and flour which had been soaked in sea water the night we landed," along with whatever seafood they could harvest. With their mother, the youngsters combed the bluffs for edible periwinkle and limpet snails. One day, a five-foot halibut washed ashore. "That night we forgot hunger as we ate pan after pan of fried halibut," Barrett recalled. Throughout the ordeal, little Flo and her brothers remained carefree and happy, entertaining themselves with stories and games of make-believe. "We children never did realize our terrible danger," she wrote.

Months passed, and *Tyee* did not return for them. When they first arrived on the island, the castaways had occasionally seen cannery boats sailing in the distance, but once winter came, there was no hope that they would be rescued. "In my mother's diary is recorded her despair when she realized that the White Chief had abandoned us to starve," Barrett wrote. In the meantime, Martin's search for gold proved fruitless.

It was not until the following June, after the family had been on the island for ten months, that a friend stopped by the trading post in Kayak and inquired about the Barretts. Hearing that they had never returned from Middleton Island, he waylaid a northbound cannery boat and went to their rescue.

Twenty-five years later, Barrett's experience on Middleton Island formed the plot for her first novel, *Where the Sun Swings North*. In the book, a family is abandoned on a deserted island by an evil "White Chief." By the end of the story, the family has discovered gold, one of the sisters has fallen in love, the castaways are rescued, and the White Chief gets the fate he deserves. Interspersed are the vivid descriptions that Barrett became known for: the sun-warmed sand emits "a perfume that is the breath of Alaska"; the sea and sky were "luminous with the rose and amethyst tinting of Alaska nights"; a passing storm produced "a hollow reverberating roll that was deep and mellow, thrilling and strange."

Even after the Barretts' terrifying experience, Martin's thirst for gold did not abate. The Klondike gold rush had begun, and shortly after the rescue, in 1897, he moved his family to Dawson City, in Canada's Yukon Territory. He found a claim near town and mined it for several years. The Barretts lived there during the summer but spent winters in Seattle, where Loll and Flo—now teenagers—attended private Catholic boarding schools.

In early 1903, Martin set his sights on Katalla, a brand-new boom-town on the south-central Alaskan coast. Deposits of coal, oil, and copper had been discovered in the area, and word had it that a railroad would soon be built through Katalla. Perhaps tired of prospecting, Martin bought a general store, a hotel, and a restaurant/saloon there, and the Barretts finally settled down. All of the family's businesses served as social centers for the community. In the hotel, the family set up Katalla's first Christmas tree and invited everyone in town to celebrate. The store, as Barrett later described it, was "the typical Alaskan trading post with a little of everything on the shelves and in the center a big stove made of a gasoline drum. About this heater every evening sit the old-timers, telling stories. . . . In our old back room we have entertained men from every walk of life, beginning with German barons and ending with Tlinget witch-doctors."

The whole family helped out with operating the businesses. At seventeen, Flo also worked as a clerk and typist in the local government office. She would live in Katalla for the next fifteen years,

Katalla, Alaska, 1907 —CIHS Reeve Collection, Anchorage Museum, AMRC-B63-X-11-3

though the town never achieved the prominence that its boosters had expected. Violent winter storms from the Gulf made boat landings difficult, keeping the town from developing as a shipping port; in addition, the oil wells soon stopped producing. Eventually the hoped-for railroad bypassed Katalla in favor of Cordova. At its 1907 peak, however, Katalla had a population of more than 5,000, with fortune-seekers coming and going virtually every day.

Among the new arrivals was former newspaper publisher Oliver Willoughby, who came to Katalla from Port Townsend, Washington, in 1906 to join his older half-brother, Charles Willoughby, in prospecting for minerals for outside investors. When Flo met Ollie, he was thirty-eight years old and she was twenty. They fell in love almost immediately and were married the following January. Not quite a year later, in December 1907, Flo delivered a stillborn baby boy. To her sorrow, she was never able to have any other children.

In 1908 Ollie opened a lumber business, where he later hired Flo's brother Lawrence to work for him. Ollie also continued to look for investors, work that often took him to the States. Meanwhile the young Mrs. Willoughby concentrated on making a home on the couple's small farm, entertaining friends, and enjoying the natural beauty around her. For the next several years, she was mostly content, though she missed her frequently absent husband.

Flo's happiness was disrupted in November 1912, when her beloved father Martin, who had meant so much to her, died of a heart attack. Only four months later, another tragedy devastated the Barrett family when twenty-year-old Fred, who was attending college in Spokane, Washington, contracted tuberculosis and died. It was a sorrowful time. That June, Flo was taken aback when her mother, only seven months a widow, eloped with Ollie's older half-brother, Charles Willoughby. The news was surprising but not displeasing, as Flo liked and respected Charles, who was now both her brother-in-law and her stepfather.

Unfortunately, Flo's own marriage was disintegrating. In July 1913 Ollie moved permanently to Port Townsend while she remained in Katalla. By this time, the boomtown was already on the decline, increasing Flo's feeling of isolation. The two kept their relationship going for several more years, writing numerous letters back and forth, but Flo actually saw her husband only about once a year. In the meantime, she kept herself busy with a new interest—writing. Over the summer in 1914, she took a correspondence course in writing and began scribbling little stories and short articles. She sold a few of the latter to magazines and newspapers.

By then, her brother Loll had married, divorced, and remarried. In 1914 he and his wife Ella had a baby girl. The child, named Florence after her grandmother and aunt, was nicknamed Beau. Twenty-five years later, Flo would model the heroine of one of her books, Sondra O'Moore, after her much-loved redheaded niece.

Over the next few years, Flo—not yet Barrett Willoughby—continued writing and published a good number of articles, mostly for the *All-Alaska Review* and *Sunset Magazine*. But with Ollie rarely home and money problems mounting, it became clear that her marriage was ending. In 1917 Oliver filed for divorce. In spite of the breakup, the two remained good friends and continued corresponding for many years.

Now divorced with no income other than the few dollars she earned writing, living in what had become little more than a ghost town, thirty-one-year-old Flo was at an impasse. In July 1917, less than three months after the divorce, she impulsively married a man named Roger Summy, a former employee of Ollie's who now lived in the growing town of Anchorage. Glad to have a new start in a larger city, Flo moved to Anchorage with her new husband.

At the time, Flo's brother Loll was also living in Anchorage, working in the oil fields while Ella and Beau stayed in the States. But shortly after Flo came to town with Roger, some trouble—in the form of a woman—led Loll to leave Alaska and move to Casper, Wyoming. After arriving in Casper in early October, he sent for his wife and daughter. Unfortunately, he soon found out that his Anchorage trouble had followed him to Wyoming.

Loll had been in Casper only a short time when the woman, an itinerant floozy named Bessie Fisher, appeared in town and confronted Loll in public a few times, accusing him of stealing her money, her jewelry, and her affections. Police arrested her, but they soon let her go after she promised to leave Casper. The day she was released, October 26, 1917, Loll Barrett and his family were having lunch at a local restaurant when an enraged Bessie appeared at their table with a gun. Without a word, she shot Loll in the torso, right in front of his wife and three-year-old child, then immediately gave herself up. Loll died in the hospital a few hours later. At her trial, Bessie claimed self-defense. The jury was deadlocked and a mistrial was declared. Bessie was never retried, and the case was eventually dismissed.

Back in Anchorage, Flo—having endured so many painful losses in a short period—struggled along. She took some college classes and continued writing, but her ill-advised marriage to Roger was failing fast. The couple separated in May 1918, only ten months after the wedding. Flo returned to Katalla, but there was little now to hold her there. At the end of the summer, she left Alaska and moved to Tacoma, Washington, where she enrolled in college and found a secretarial job at a law firm. She was busy but not fullfilled—she longed to become a real writer. An author friend suggested she go to San Francisco, where she'd have more opportunities to meet people in publishing.

By January 1920, Flo was living in San Francisco. She loved the city and found it inspiring—her head, she recalled, was "full of story plots." Within a few months she had found a job as a secretary for an author and reviewer named Frederick O'Brien. He encouraged her to write, advising her to "Be yourself and keep a diary." She published several more articles and began working on her first novel, a story that had swirled in her head for many years. Based on her childhood experience on Middleton Island, *Where the Sun Swings North* was published in 1922. It was the first time Flo used her pen name, Barrett Willoughby. O'Brien had advised her to use a masculine-sounding name; it was common in those days for female authors to use male pen names so their work would be taken more seriously. Indeed, readers often assumed she was a man. Before long, Flo was going by the name Barrett in her personal life as well, and friends began calling her "Barrie."

Where the Sun Swings North was an immediate success. National reviews were mixed, but Alaskans themselves embraced the novel, praising its authenticity. The *Sitka Review* said it "breathes the real Alaskan spirit," and the *Pathfinder* said it was "truer to Alaska and its people than any novel that has yet been published." Another reviewer wrote, "She succeeds in communicating to her readers the full flavor of this country. . . . Barrett Willoughby is worth watching. More power to her pen!" With her first book, Barrett was already being hailed as the "first real Alaskan novelist."

Upon completion of her first novel, Barrett wasted no time in beginning her second one. She traveled to Kodiak to visit a fox farm, which was to be the new book's setting. Although all of Barrett's novels were set in Alaska, interestingly, she did no actual writing in the Northland. She traveled there for inspiration and research but did all her writing in San Francisco. She later explained why: "Up there I am too busy and too happy just living." She also felt she needed a little distance from her subject before she could write about it. For this reason, Barrett never moved back to Alaska permanently. Instead, for the rest of her life, she would travel back and forth between her heart's two homes—California and Alaska.

Barrett found the old Russian town of Kodiak to be "like living in a delightful, old-world fairy tale." Continuing to the fox farm on a nearby island—called Rocking Moon Island in the book—she spent two months getting to know the landscape, the fur business, and the foxes themselves. "We could imitate their barks," she wrote. "We 'talked fox' to those interested little animals perched on driftwood."

The novel, entitled *Rocking Moon*, not only told a story of romance and suspense, it also reflected Barrett's fascination with the Russian history of Kodiak. As one reviewer noted, "Tenderly, lovingly, Barrett Willoughby picked up bits of [Russian] legend

Barrett shows Alaskan artifacts to Rockcliffe Fellowes and Laska Winter, stars of Rocking Moon, *the silent film version of her 1925 novel.* —Barrett Willoughby Papers, UAF-1972-116-292, Archives, University of Alaska Fairbanks

and history and wove them into the background of her novel." She dedicated the book to Russian Orthodox priest Fr. Andrew Peter Kashevaroff, who had spent his entire life in Alaska and was an expert in its history. *Rocking Moon*, published in April 1925, was so popular that by September it was already in its fifth printing.

No sooner was *Rocking Moon* released than Hollywood came knocking. Metropolitan Pictures, a leading Hollywood studio, contracted to make a silent film version of the novel. It would be the first movie ever filmed on location in Alaska, in this case a fox farm near Sitka. Barrett met with the film's producers and stars in California, but she did not go to Alaska with them and played no active part in the production. Released in 1926, at the end of the silent-movie era, the picture was modestly successful.

Around the time Barrett finished *Rocking Moon*, her mother and stepfather, Florence and Charles Willoughby, gave up on the dying town of Katalla and moved into Barrie's spacious split-level home in San Carlos, near San Francisco. Barrie continued publishing magazine articles, many of them profiles of interesting Alaskans. Some of these, along with a few previously unpublished pieces, were collected in her first nonfiction book, *Gentlemen Unafraid*, published in 1928. The book included first-person accounts of six Alaska adventurers, accompanied by some seventy-five black-and-white photographs Barrett had taken. One of the men she wrote about was her father, Martin Barrett. Others included explorer Alexander "Sandy" Smith, dogsled racer Allan Alexander "Scotty" Allan, and steamboat captain Sydney Barrington. Like her fiction, the book was full of adventure, romance, and lyrical descriptions of Alaska's natural beauty.

In the meantime, after nearly ten years of being single, Barrie fell in love once again. On October 19, 1927, she married Robert (Bob) Prosser, an engineer at the University of California. Sadly, this marriage, too, would end after a brief period of happiness, but not in divorce. Eight months after the wedding, Bob went into the hospital for a sinus operation. The surgery did not go well, and he died from complications on the operating table on June 9, 1928.

As in the past, Barrett coped with her grief by throwing herself into her work. Her next project was a novel entitled *The Trail Eater: A Romance of the All-Alaska Sweepstakes*. The subtitle refers to a

Barrett and her mother on a research trip, standing with three unidentified men before Native totem poles, probably in Sitka or Ketchikan, circa late 1920s
—Barrett Willoughby Papers, UAF-1972-116-274, Archives, University of Alaska Fairbanks

four-hundred-mile dogsled race that was held annually in Alaska, a forerunner to the modern Iditarod races. The hero of the book was based on Scotty Allan, the racer Barrett had profiled in *Gentlemen Unafraid*. *The Trail Eater* was published in 1929 to wide critical acclaim.

The following year, Barrett's second nonfiction book, *Sitka: Portal to Romance*, was published. A combination of history and memoir, the book traces Sitka's past in much detail while also sharing the author's own recollections of the Sitka she knew as a child and her impressions upon revisiting it many years later. "To know Alaska one must first know Sitka," Barrett wrote in the introduction.

Like Barrett's other nonfiction work, *Sitka* won praise, but it was her novels that readers gobbled up. *Spawn of the North*, published in 1932, became her most popular book yet. So many people were eager to read Barrett Willoughby's next book, it went into a third printing even before its official publication date. This novel, set in Ketchikan, involved fish pirates, fierce storms, and, of course, the romantic entanglements of a brave young heroine.

As with *Rocking Moon*, Hollywood bought the movie rights to *Spawn of the North*. This film, produced by Paramount Studios, was a major motion picture featuring some of the biggest stars of the day—Henry Fonda, Dorothy Lamour, John Barrymore, and George Raft. During the filming, the producers experienced numerous difficulties and delays, and they ended up filming most of the picture in California rather than on location in Ketchikan. But when *Spawn of the North* was at last released in 1938, it opened to so much enthusiasm that two women were injured in the crush of a crowd awaiting the film's preview in California. The movie was successful with the critics as well: one praised its "authentic photographic record of Alaska life and customs" and its "highly interesting views of Indian rituals as the spawning season begins." The film even won an Academy Award for its sound and visual effects.

By the time the movie came out, Barrett had published two more books and several magazine articles. She had also married once again. Her fourth husband was an Alaskan boat pilot and good friend named Larry O'Connor, who had followed her from Wrangell to California. After several years of courting her, Larry

Spawn of the North *(1932), one of Barrett's most popular books, was made into a major motion picture in 1938.*

finally persuaded Barrett to become Mrs. O'Connor on July 17, 1935. He moved into Barrie's house in San Carlos, where her mother and stepfather Charles Willoughby continued to live in the apartment below the main floor. Barrie set her new husband up in business, buying a furniture store for him to run.

Like Barrett's father Martin, Larry was an adventurous free spirit. He was also an aspiring author. For the first several years of the marriage, Larry and Barrie had fun traveling together and helping each other with their writing. Barrett was at the peak of her success, and life was going quite well for her.

The book that followed *Spawn of the North* was a nonfiction work, *Alaskans All*, published in 1933. Similar to *Gentlemen Unafraid*, it was a collection of profiles of interesting Alaskans. The book featured the stories of four men—including bush pilot Carl (Ben) Eielson, who became a good friend of Barrie's—and one woman, innkeeper Harriet Pullen.

In her research for *Alaskans All*, Barrett became particularly enthralled with Ben Eielson. Upon their first meeting, when Barrie mentioned that she had never been up in a plane before, Ben immediately offered to take her for a ride, and she immediately accepted the invitation. A few days later, the intrepid Barrett was soaring over Fairbanks in Ben's open-cockpit biplane. It was, she recalled, "a glorious experience." She subsequently accompanied Ben on several more flights, each one an adventure in itself. In a talk she gave when the book came out, Barrett described one of her most memorable trips with Ben, when they were caught in bad weather flying over the Endicott Mountains:

> For four hours I watched Ben flying blind in a blowing Bering Sea fog so thick I could scarcely see the tips of our wings. . . . Ben's manipulation of the plane was such that nothing that may come to me now can ever equal the wild exultation, the sense of cosmic freedom I experienced while he beat about like a trapped

bird among the hidden peaks, climbing, side-slipping, banking to avoid those cold menacing crags that kept rushing at us out of the vapor.

As it turned out, this flight was the last one she ever shared with her friend. Two weeks later, while on a rescue flight to save an ice-bound ship in Siberia, Ben crashed his plane and was killed. As Barrett sadly observed, "At the height of his fame, Ben Eielson's gallant spirit went on over the horizon into the last Great Unknown." Years later, in collaboration with fellow author Edna Chandler, Barrett would write a children's book about Ben entitled *Pioneer of Alaskan Skies.*

Barrett's next book after *Alaskans All* was a novel called *River House*, published in 1936. Another romantic adventure story, this one was set in Wrangell, where the mysteriously powerful Stikine River was almost a character in itself. Another huge success for Barrett, *River House* was reprinted three times in its first month.

Two years after *River House* was published, as Barrett was working on her next novel, her stepfather, Charles Willoughby, died of heart failure. Her mother Florence continued to live with her until Florence's own death in the 1950s. For all her impetuousness, Barrett was steadfast in her devotion to her family, including her niece, Beau, whom Barrett had taken care of for a while after Lawrence's murder. Their relationship remained strong over the years, and Barrett based the heroine of her next book, *Sondra O'Moore*, on the red-haired Beau. Published in 1939, the novel was set in Sitka, the place Barrett knew and loved so well. Like her previous fiction, *Sondra O'Moore* was a bestseller.

Next came another nonfiction work, *Alaska Holiday*, published in 1940. This book contained several stories that had previously been published in magazines, along with new material. The pieces covered a variety of topics, among them caribou, lighthouses, totem poles, and seal colonies. In one section, Barrett described her own adventures in Kodiak; other pieces profiled notable Alaskans, including dancehall entertainer Kathleen "Klondike Kate" Rockwell.

Although Barrett's books sold very well, financial problems had plagued her throughout her career. Neither she nor any of her husbands were good at managing money. Larry, in particular, was a gambler and a spendthrift. He was also—as Barrie eventually discovered—repeatedly unfaithful to her. In 1942 he ran off with the bookkeeper of the furniture store Barrett had bought for him. Thus ended her fourth marriage. After the divorce, she found that she had little money left. Incredibly, she felt "no resentment against Larry," she said in a letter to Beau. "He gave me great happiness for awhile—but I imagine he got tired."

By this time, the United States was involved in World War II. After the Japanese invasion of the Aleutian Islands, traveling to Alaska was essentially out of the question. But Barrett was not ready to give up writing, and she needed income. During the war years she wrote what would be her final published novel, *The Golden Totem*, which took place in Juneau. Its dedication revealed Barrett's own state of mind—disheartened yet unshakably optimistic: "To a cheerful, disenchanted lady—myself."

Published in 1945, *The Golden Totem* was, fortunately, another success, but not so fortunately, it was destined to be her last. Barrett's style of writing was becoming outdated, and the mystery of Alaska was fading as transportation advances were making the territory more easily accessible. In the years following *The Golden Totem*, Barrett continued writing, but she was able to publish only an occasional article. To make a living, she moved to Los Angeles and took temporary jobs assisting other writers with their stories and scripts. She brought her aging mother with her to L.A. The elder Florence became ill, and she died in Los Angeles sometime in the early to mid-1950s.

Barrett Willoughby, circa early 1950s

In late 1956, after her mother's death, Barrie happily moved back to San Francisco. Alone now at age seventy, she put her house in San Carlos up for sale and moved into an apartment in downtown San Francisco. She kept writing and planned several book projects, but none materialized except a short biography of her friend, aviator Ben Eielson. Written with a coauthor, Edna Walker Chandler, the book was called *Pioneer of Alaskan Skies: The Story of Ben Eielson.* Shortly before it was published in the fall of 1959, Barrett became ill and was hospitalized in Berkeley. On July 29, 1959,

Barrett Willoughby, age seventy-three, died of heart failure. Her niece Beau said that at the time of her death, she had been taking a writing class. Like her heroines, Barrett never gave up.

Florence Barrett Willoughby was a hardworking, adventurous, and passionate woman who endured many heartbreaks and disappointments yet remained unwaveringly hopeful and positive. As Beau remembered, "she never missed an opportunity to show her love for family and friends." Indeed, Barrett Willoughby was driven by love, not only for her own family and friends, but also for a certain special place. Through her writing, Barrett showed the world a different side of Alaska—her Alaska. In contrast to its image as a cold, dark, and desolate land, Barrett dedicated herself to revealing its incomparable beauty, rich history, and diverse culture.

> There's something in the air up there—a sense of expectancy that is the very essence of youth and romance. When you wake up in the morning—no matter how old you are—you have that feeling you had when a child: "Something wonderful is going to happen today."

ELIZABETH PERATROVICH

"The Martin Luther King of Alaska"

February 5, 1945, dawned gray and drizzly in southeastern Alaska. That morning, thirty-four-year-old Elizabeth Peratrovich was busily preparing herself and her five-year-old daughter, Loretta, for a special outing. After checking her appearance in the mirror, she put on her raincoat and helped Loretta into hers, picked up her knitting bag, and set off for the territorial capitol in Juneau, where she would wait for her turn to speak before the legislators. Would her years-long effort to pass a law banning discrimination against Native Alaskans finally pay off? Elizabeth did not know it, but she was about to step into history.

Elizabeth Jean Wanamaker was born to a Tlingit mother on July 4, 1911, in Petersburg, Alaska. At birth she was given the Tlingit name of Kaaxgal.aat. When she was a just a baby, a local Tlingit couple, Andrew and Jean Wanamaker, adopted her and named her Elizabeth. The Wanamakers, who had no other children, served as Presbyterian missionaries for the fishing villages on the various islands of southeastern Alaska's Alexander Archipelago.

Elizabeth spent her early years in Petersburg before starting high school at Sheldon Jackson School (which eventually became

Elizabeth (left) with her parents, Andrew and Jean Wanamaker, in Klawock, 1927 —Courtesy Roy Peratrovich Jr.

Sheldon Jackson College) in Sitka. In 1928 the Wanamaker family moved south to Ketchikan, where Elizabeth finished high school. It was there she met her future husband, the handsome and popular Roy Peratrovich. Like Elizabeth, Roy was of Tlingit heritage. His mother, Mary Skan, was Tlingit and his father, John, was an immigrant from the country that later became Yugoslavia (then part of the Austrian Empire). Of John Peratrovich's ten children, Roy was the youngest boy, born in Klawock in 1908.

Like many other Alaskan students in those days, both Roy and Elizabeth graduated late from high school; Roy was twenty-three and Elizabeth was nineteen. After their graduation in 1931, they both went to Bellingham, Washington, to attend Washington State Normal School, a teacher's college (now part of Western Washington University). By then, the United States was in the midst of the Great Depression, and the two took whatever part-time jobs they could find to pay college costs and living expenses. When the semester was over, in December 1931, Roy and Elizabeth married. "We were both broke," Roy later laughed, "and decided that two can live as cheaply as one."

Immediately after the wedding, the Peratroviches moved back to Klawock, where Roy worked as a fish buyer and boat captain at a cannery. During the next decade, the couple's three children were born. Roy Jr. (born 1934), Frank (born 1937), and Loretta (born 1940) grew up in a home that they remembered as happy and busy. Roy Jr., the eldest, recalled, "Mom and Dad . . . didn't have a lot of money, but we always had something to eat and an open door for friends."

In Klawock the Peratroviches were very active in the community. They were especially involved in the Alaska Native Brotherhood (ANB) organization, founded in Sitka in 1912, and its women's counterpart, the Alaska Native Sisterhood (ANS), founded three years later. Elizabeth's own father, Andrew Wanamaker, was a charter member of the ANB and was named an honorary founder. The organization's main goals were to end discrimination against Native Alaskans and to preserve Native cultures. By the 1930s the ANB and ANS had chapters throughout southeastern Alaska and had gained considerable political power.

After working in the cannery for a few years, Roy began working for the local government of Klawock, serving as a city clerk, police officer, city judge, and postmaster. In 1936 he was elected mayor of Klawock and served four terms, which ended in 1940. In addition, in 1940 Roy was chosen as the Grand President of the ANB—a position he held until 1945. For her part, Elizabeth served as Grand Vice President of the ANS from 1941 to 1942 and as Grand President from 1945 to 1946.

In 1941 the Peratrovich family moved to the territorial capital of Juneau—Roy and Elizabeth felt that, as leaders of a major political organization, they would be more effective living near the seat of the territorial government. The Peratroviches also looked forward to a better quality of life and better schools for their children, which the larger city presumably offered.

Roy accepted a job at the capitol, working for the territorial government's revenue department. The family started looking for a home to buy or rent close to Roy's new workplace. But the Peratroviches were unprepared for what they discovered in the capital city. They began to notice that many Juneau businesses displayed signs that said "Whites Only" or "No Indians or Dogs Allowed." When Elizabeth found a nice house in a pleasant neighborhood and inquired about renting it, she was told that the owners rented only to whites, not Natives. The family was advised to seek housing in one of the city's Native neighborhoods, where most of the homes were substandard in quality. This outrageous discrimination solidified Roy and Elizabeth's determination to change things in Alaska.

When the Peratroviches finally did find a home, they became one of the first Native families in Juneau to live in a non-Native neighborhood. In 1941 Roy Jr. became the first Native child in Alaska to attend an integrated public school; Frank and Loretta followed. Until that time, the public schools in Alaska were segregated, and Native children were expected to attend an "Indian" school, where the quality of education was considered to be inferior. The

Peratrovich children themselves were mostly unaware of the racial tensions in Juneau in the early days. As Roy Jr. later put it, "I just lived to play basketball."

When the United States entered World War II in December 1941, it became apparent that the army also practiced racial discrimination. Although Native and white soldiers in Alaska served in the same units, all soldiers, regardless of race, were forbidden to have personal contact with Native women, even family members. At dances sponsored by the USO, for example, Native servicemen were welcome, but Native women were not admitted. Similarly in restaurants and movie theaters, Native men in uniform were allowed to sit in the whites-only seats, but Native women were not.

From the kitchen table in their home, the Peratroviches launched a campaign to expose and eliminate such bigotry, writing letters and attending legislative meetings. In a December 30, 1941, letter to territorial governor Ernest Gruening, they pointed out the injustice of segregationist policies:

> My attention has been called to a business establishment in Douglas, namely, "Douglas Inn," which has a sign on the door which reads, "No Natives Allowed." In view of the present emergency [i.e., the war], when unity is being stressed, don't you think that it is very Un-American? We have always contended that we are entitled to every benefit accorded our so-called White Brothers. We pay the required taxes, taxes in some instances that we feel are unjust, such as the school tax. Our Native people pay the school tax each year to educate the white children, yet they try to exclude our children from these schools.

Elizabeth and the ANS also took Juneau's *Daily Alaska Empire* to task when they learned that the newspaper had different standards for reporting on the arrests of white and Native minors. If the offenders were Indian, their names and ages were published, but if they were white, their identities were withheld. Visiting the newspaper's offices in person, the ANS members demanded that the *Daily Alaska Empire* give Native juveniles the same protections as white ones.

These local efforts produced some results, but to counter discrimination on a broad scale, the activists realized they needed legislative action. The ANB and the ANS found supporters within the government, especially Governor Gruening and Anthony Dimond, Alaska's territorial delegate to the U.S. Congress. With their help, members of the ANB and the ANS—led by Roy and Elizabeth Peratrovich—drew up a legislative proposal, and Senator Norman Walker introduced it in the Alaska Legislature in 1943.

The proposed law would prohibit discriminatory practices in virtually all public and private institutions. Businesses could no longer display "No Indians" signs; selling or renting housing only to whites would be illegal; non-whites could not be refused service on public or commercial transportation; and all public places would be open to everyone. The 1943 bill did not provide for the integration of elementary schools, however, since public schools were operated under federal jurisdiction, meaning territorial law could not be applied. Nevertheless, if the measure was approved, it would be the first antidiscrimination legislation in the territorial United States.

Elizabeth, with little Loretta in tow, attended every session to hear the senators debate and help lobby for the bill. Loretta remembered running between seats in the gallery while her mother sat knitting and listening attentively to the proceedings. Roy, as president of the ANB, was the only citizen called to testify.

Much of the testimony given by the bill's opponents was appallingly racist. Some senators asserted that Natives had not attained a level of culture sophisticated enough to be considered a "civilized" people. Hearing this, Roy wondered privately how they defined "civilized." He remarked, "Looking over the court record in Alaska, one wonders if the white man is really civilized."

The vote was expected to be close, and indeed, it was a tie. To pass, however, the bill needed a majority vote, so the measure failed. Governor Gruening said, "While I am greatly disappointed in this result and consider it shocking that . . . the Alaska legislature should put itself on record before the whole world as in favor of discrimination . . . the outcome was a good deal closer than I would have expected." In spite of this setback, the governor declared, he was optimistic about the future of the movement. Even though it did not pass, the bill's introduction brought the problem to light. Gruening believed that its very failure would inspire Native Alaskans to become more involved in the political process.

The governor's prediction proved to be correct. In 1944 Roy's brother, Frank Peratrovich, was elected to the legislature. He and some other new members supported the fight to make racial discrimination illegal. Further support came from an unexpected source. In February 1944, fifteen-year-old Alberta Schenck, an Inupiaq usher at Nome's Dream Theater, protested her employer's segregation policy and was immediately fired. Afterward, she wrote an open letter to the *Nome Nugget* decrying the indignity of such policies. Later she and a friend, a white army sergeant, came to the theater and sat in the whites-only section. Alberta was removed from her seat, arrested, and jailed overnight. She then wrote a letter describing the incident to Governor Gruening, who made her story public with a promise to redouble his efforts to combat racism. As the news of this defiant teenager spread, public support for civil-rights reform swelled.

At the next assemby of the territorial legislature in February 1945, a new antidiscrimination bill was introduced. It passed the House of Representatives, but it faced angry opposition in the Senate. What happened next was, as one historian called it, "one of the most dramatic confrontations in Alaska political history."

The capitol gallery was packed with spectators. On the floor, many senators argued against the proposal. Tolbert Scott of Nome believed the bill would encourage intermarriage, increasing "the mixed-breed problem." Anchorage senator Gerald Collins agreed and added that in his opinion, Native Americans wanted to remain separate from the whites. Senator Frank Whaley of Fairbanks remarked that he did not want to sit next to an Eskimo in a movie theater because they did not bathe often enough. Juneau senator Allen Shattuck also weighed in: "Far from being brought closer together, the races should be kept farther apart," he declared. "Who are these people, barely out of savagery, who want to associate with us whites with 5,000 years of recorded civilization behind us?"

In the gallery, Elizabeth sat quietly, knitting and listening, until the legislators of the mostly white, all-male Senate finished their testimony. When the public was invited to speak, she put her knitting down, stood up, and announced that she would like to be heard.

In the Tlingit culture, the ability to speak well is a highly regarded skill, and it was one that Elizabeth Peratrovich possessed in abundance. Her confidence was unshakable, and she never hesitated to stand up and talk. Attractive, poised, and neatly dressed, she has been described as "regal" in appearance. As one friend put it, "She had a presence about her."

Elizabeth was the only private citizen to address the assembly that day. At the podium, in a clear and steady voice, she began: "I would not have expected that I, who am barely out of savagery, would have to remind gentlemen with 5,000 years of recorded civilization behind them of our Bill of Rights."

She went on to describe incidents of racial discrimination she had observed, including some of her own personal experiences:

> When my husband and I came to Juneau and sought a home in
> a nice neighborhood where our children could play happily with
> our neighbors' children, we found such a house and arranged to

lease it. When the owners learned we were Indians, they said no. Would we be compelled to live in the slums?

The senators questioned Elizabeth for two hours. At one point, Senator Shattuck asked her if the proposed law would eliminate discrimination. "Have you eliminated larceny or murder by passing a law against it?" she retorted. "No law will eliminate crimes, but at least you as legislators can assert to the world that you recognize the evil of the present situation and speak your intent to help us overcome discrimination."

Governor Gruening signs the Antidiscrimination Bill, 1945. Elizabeth is standing to the governor's left; Roy is on the far right. —Courtesy Alaska State Library, Alaska Territorial Governors Photographs Collection, ASL-P274-1-2

At this, her final point, the room broke into loud applause. Three days later, on February 8, 1945, the Alaska Anti-discrimination Act passed the Senate by a vote of 11 to 5. It was signed into law by Governor Gruening on February 16. That night, Elizabeth and Roy, who had worked side by side to end discrimination, danced in celebration in the ballroom of the Baranof Hotel, a place that had previously been closed to Natives.

Over this period of the early 1940s, Roy served in various posts with Alaska's territorial treasury department, while Elizabeth worked as a clerk in the same department. During the war, Elizabeth led fundraising efforts for the American Red Cross. Shortly after the anti-discrimination law passed, Roy took a new position as a financial officer for the Alaska Native Service, then under the management of the federal Bureau of Indian Affairs (BIA), while Elizabeth began working for the Territorial Vocational Rehabilitation Department. Throughout the years in Juneau, Elizabeth remained active with the ANS and the community. She "never stopped trying to correct a wrong," Roy Jr. recalled. He remembered driving with her each Thanksgiving and Christmas to deliver food to needy families.

In 1952 Roy won a fellowship to study banking in Denver, Colorado, for a year, so the Peratroviches moved to Denver. There Roy worked at a local bank and took business classes at the University of Denver. Roy Jr., a senior in high school at the time, remembered studying alongside his dad at the dining room table. After Roy Jr. graduated from high school the following spring, Elizabeth and the children returned to Juneau while Roy pursued another new opportunity—he had received a United Nations scholarship to study fisheries and co-op canneries in Nova Scotia for the summer. At the end of the summer, Roy returned to his job at Alaska Native Services in Juneau and Roy Jr. left for college at the University of Washington in Seattle.

The Peratrovich family on vacation in Seattle, 1945. Back row, left to right, Roy, Roy Jr. (age fifteen), Frank (age twelve), and Elizabeth; front, Loretta (age nine) and Roy's sister Bertha Gartley. —Courtesy Roy Peratrovich Jr.

In 1955 yet another opportunity for Roy opened up. He was offered a position as the district superintendent of the Bureau of Indian Affairs in Anadarko, Oklahoma, so the family packed up and moved once again. While living in Oklahoma, Elizabeth traveled to Nashville, Tennessee, to attend a month-long conference on adult Indian education at Fisk University. One of the speakers there was Dr. Martin Luther King Jr. "She was impressed by him," her son Frank recalled. Elizabeth would undoubtedly have been surprised to know that she would someday be considered "the Martin Luther King of Alaska." Although Elizabeth's fight for equality for Native Alaskans took place two decades before Dr. King's crusade for black equality, the comparison is not unwarranted. Like Dr. King, Elizabeth was a gifted speaker and dedicated organizer who devoted her life to battling injustice.

It was while the family was in Oklahoma that Elizabeth discovered she had breast cancer. She was treated with surgery and radiation, but her cancer did not respond to the treatments. "I think my parents knew her cancer was terminal," Roy Jr. said, "so they moved back to Juneau" in 1956, after Frank graduated from high school. Roy returned to his old position as a loan officer for the BIA. Although she was sick, Elizabeth took a job at the Juneau Credit Association, perhaps to keep herself busy.

In 1957 Roy Jr., who had remained in Seattle, graduated from college and got married. In July 1958, Roy and Elizabeth's much-anticipated first grandchild, Michael, was born. Frank, meanwhile, had joined the Marine Corps. The following September, Elizabeth moved to Seattle for treatments while Roy stayed in Juneau with Loretta, then a senior in high school. Finally, on December 1, 1958, Elizabeth Peratrovich, age forty-seven, died in Seattle. Her remains were returned to Juneau for burial.

After Elizabeth's death, Roy continued to work for the Bureau of Indian Affairs in Juneau until 1968, when he moved to Anchorage. He retired from the BIA in 1983 and returned to Juneau the following year. Also in 1983 Roy was named Grand President Emeritus of the Alaska Native Brotherhood.

Although Elizabeth was well known and much beloved in her community, official statewide recognition of her contributions to Alaska did not come until 1988, when the Alaska legislature established February 16 as "Elizabeth Peratrovich Day." It was on that date in 1945 that Governor Gruening signed the antidiscrimination bill, the first law of its kind in the United States. The first celebration would take place a year later, on February 16, 1989. Her husband Roy looked forward to that first commemoration of Elizabeth Peratrovich Day, but sadly, he did not live to see the celebration. He died in Juneau on February 7, a week before the event took place. He was eighty years old.

Poster created for Elizabeth Peratrovich Day, designed by Alaska artist Apayo Moore, Alaska Native Arts Foundation —Courtesy Roy Peratrovich Jr.

Acknowledgement of Elizabeth's accomplishments continued to grow in the decades after her death. Also in 1988, the ANS established the Elizabeth Peratrovich Award to recognize achievements in Native Alaskan issues. In 1992, at the suggestion of Fran Ulmer, a co-sponsor of the Elizabeth Peratrovich Day bill four years earlier, one of the two galleries in the state House of Representatives (the one she sat in in 1945) was named after Elizabeth. At the dedication, Ulmer said, "In naming Gallery B for Elizabeth, we honor her today for her vision, her wisdom, and her courage in speaking out for what she believed to be right. . . . She reminds us that a single person, speaking from the heart, can affect the future of all Alaskans."

In 2004 Alaska senator Lisa Murkowski sponsored legislation to award a posthumous Congressional Gold Medal to both Elizabeth and Roy Peratrovich in "long overdue recognition" of their contributions to the nation's civil-rights movement. Senator Murkowski said, "There is an important lesson to be learned from the battles of Elizabeth and Roy Peratrovich. Even in defeat, they knew that change would come from their participation in our political system. They were not discouraged by their defeat in 1943. They came back fighting and enjoyed the fruits of their victory two years later."

Elizabeth was also immortalized in the arts. A one-act play about her life and work, entitled *When My Spirit Raised Its Hands: The Story of Elizabeth Peratrovich and Alaska Civil Rights*, by Tlingit actress and writer Diane Benson debuted in Anchorage in 2001. Eight years later, Benson played the role of Elizabeth in a feature-length docudrama called *For the Rights of All: Ending Jim Crow in Alaska* by Alaskan filmmaker Jeffry Silverman. The film was shown on PBS stations nationwide, and it is still sometimes screened at various events throughout Alaska. The arts also play a large role in the annual celebration of Elizabeth Peratrovich Day. Each year, the day is observed with education and art programs; in 2014 the Alaska Native Arts Foundation in Anchorage organized a show of works by Alaskan women artists to honor the occasion.

Perhaps the most personal tributes to Elizabeth and Roy were created by their eldest son. After retiring as a structural engineer in 1999, Roy Jr. became a sculptor, specializing in cast-metal bronzes. In 2002 he donated the two bronze busts he crafted of his parents to the National Museum of the American Indian in Washington, D.C. In addition, a copy of the Elizabeth bust is displayed in the foyer of the state capitol in Juneau.

Roy Jr. began working on another sculpture honoring his parents after the 2003 dedication of Peratrovich Park, a small park in

Bronze busts of Roy and Elizabeth Peratrovich, created by Roy Peratrovich Jr. in 2002 —Courtesy Roy Peratrovich Jr.

downtown Anchorage that was renamed for Roy and Elizabeth at the urging of the Alaska Native Center. The result of Roy Jr.'s four-year effort, a ten-foot mixed-material sculpture called *Flight of the Raven*, was unveiled in Peratrovich Park in 2008. According to Tlingit legend, the Raven brought light to the world when he stole the sun and gave it to the people. Here the Raven represents Elizabeth, who was born into the Raven clan, and the sculpture symbolizes another way in which the Raven brought light to the world.

MAHALA ASHLEY DICKERSON

"Equality and Justice"

One of the many pictures of renowned Alaska attorney Mahala Ashley Dickerson shows her in her eighties, sitting with another well-dressed elderly black woman. The woman is her childhood friend and classmate, Rosa Parks, who grew up to become a more famous civil-rights leader than Mahala herself. The picture was taken at Mahala's Matanuska-Susitna (Mat-Su) Valley homestead near Wasilla in 1996, when Rosa came to visit her old friend from Alabama. In some ways, the photo represents the full circle of Mahala's journey from her girlhood in the segregated South to her later life as a pioneer lawyer in the far north, where she continued to practice law into her nineties. Like Rosa, Mahala dedicated her entire life and career to fighting bigotry and discrimination.

Before moving to Alaska in 1958, at age forty-six, Mahala had already built up an impressive record of accomplishments. Born and raised in rural Alabama, she had gone to college, earned a law degree, and become the first black female attorney to be admitted into the Alabama Bar Association (1948). A few years later she became the second black woman to practice in Indiana and to be

Rosa Parks (left) visits her childhood friend, Mahala Dickerson, in 1996 —Photo by Erik Hill,*Anchorage Daily News* Archives, courtesy Gruscana, Flickr Creative Commons

admitted into the Indiana Bar Association (1952). She was also the mother of triplet sons, born in 1939.

In Alaska, Mahala added many other "firsts" to her life story. She became the first black homesteader in the Mat-Su Valley and the first black attorney of either sex to be admitted to the Alaska Bar Association (1959) and to practice in Alaska. Years later, in 1983, she was the first African American to serve as president of the National Association of Women Lawyers. In additon, she received numerous awards and honors during her life, among them the NAACP Freedom Award in 1982, a Zeta Phi Beta Award in 1985, an honorary doctorate from the University of Alaska in 1994, and the National Bar Association's Margaret Brent Award in 1995. Even after her death in 2007, she was honored, inducted into the Alaska Women's Hall of Fame in 2009.

But long before the awards, a monthlong vacation trip in the summer of 1958 first brought Mahala to Alaska while it was still a territory. It was not a place she had ever thought of living, but she fell in love at first sight. The day after her arrival in Anchorage, she signed up for a homestead in the nearby Mat-Su Valley. Upon returning to Indiana, she packed up her belongings and headed north, where she would remain for the rest of her life.

Anchorage, Alaska, is 4,300 miles from Montgomery, Alabama, where Mahala Alice Ashley was born on October 12, 1912. She was the second of three daughters born to John Augustine Ashley and Hattie Ethel Moss Ashley. Both of her parents had been school-teachers; John was also a farmer, the proprietor of a general store, and an insurance salesman. Two of Mahala's grandparents had been born into slavery.

In the autobiography Mahala wrote later in life, *Delayed Justice for Sale*, she told of her early childhood on the farm with her sisters, Erna and Harriet. The Ashleys were not wealthy, but they always had plenty to eat. Mahala described watching wagons bringing bacon, molasses, and flour to her father's store. She remembered having tubs of ripe peaches, which she so loved to eat, along with orchards of pecan and fruit trees, fields of vegetables, and a yard full of chickens. The family even had a car—one of the first in town. It was only when she was older that she became aware of the difficulties facing black families in the early-twentieth-century South.

Mahala's parents, former teachers, read aloud to their girls, recited poetry, sang songs, and emphasized the value of education. Mahala credited them for her lifelong love of books. In those days, the public schools, like most public places in the American South, were segregated; that is, there were separate schools for white and black children. In Mahala's farming community, the only school for African American children was a poorly equipped one-room schoolhouse, and education ended after the eighth grade. Buses transported white children to their school; black children walked. Mahala's older sister, Erna, attended the public school for a few years, but John and Hattie wanted better opportunities for their daughters. When Mahala was seven, they enrolled her and Erna in a nearby private school, the famous Montgomery Industrial School for Girls, better known as "Mrs. White's school." Later, Harriet also attended the school, as did several of Mahala's cousins.

The school was founded in 1886 by Alice White and H. Margaret Beard, two northern white women who wanted to provide southern black children with both an education and a sense of pride. An outgrowth of the American Missionary Association's schools for black children in the South, Mrs. White's school stressed not only academics and vocational training but also Christian morality. The school's 325 students, who wore uniforms to class, studied reading, writing, and mathematics along with practical skills such as sewing, cooking, and health.

Like its founders, the school's ten teachers were all northern white women. While the black community welcomed and appreciated the teachers, they were resented and scorned by the white citizens of Montgomery. Twice during the forty-one years it operated, the school was burned by arsonists. In an era when fewer than 7 percent of African Americans graduated from high school, Mrs. White's school played a vital role in shaping the lives of these rural black girls, and many of its graduates—including Rosa McCauley Parks— later became activists in the civil-rights movement of the 1960s.

Mahala loved school and made straight A's. She particularly loved the school library, where she could choose as many books as she wanted to read over the weekends. "I would always hide in a little corner with my books and had built for myself a private world," she wrote, adding that "my chores in the family suffered as a result." Mahala especially enjoyed the classic children's literature of the day, such as *Pollyanna*, *Anne of Green Gables*, and *Little Women*.

When Mahala was in the fourth grade, a new girl entered her class. Her name was Rosa McCauley, and she and Mahala became close friends. Decades later, as Rosa Parks, she would become known as "the first lady of civil rights" after she broke the law in 1955 by refusing to give up her seat on a public bus to a white passenger. Rosa was arrested and fired from her job, but her act of defiance became a symbol of the emerging civil-rights movement. She worked closely with a local minister named Rev. Dr. Martin Luther King Jr. to organize the citywide Montgomery bus boycott of 1955–56. Rosa's lifetime of activism earned her many honors, including the Presidential Medal of Freedom. Rosa credited Mrs. White's school with teaching her that she "was a person with dignity and self-respect who should not set my sights lower than anyone else because I was black."

After attending the public high school in Montgomery for a year and the high school at Alabama State Teacher's College for the remaining three, Mahala won a scholarship to attend Fisk University in Nashville, Tennessee. She described entering Fisk as "a dream come true." Like Mrs. White's school, Fisk University was founded by the American Missionary Association after the Civil War. The school was "open to all, regardless of race," with academic offerings "of the highest standards." By the time Mahala enrolled, the university had overcome years of struggle and uncertainty to become a leader in the education of African Americans. In 1935 she graduated cum laude. Although her grades qualified her for membership in the national scholastic honorary society Phi Beta Kappa, black students were excluded from joining in those days. Mahala would finally be awarded a membership key fifty years later.

After graduating from Fisk in 1935, Mahala returned to Alabama. She intended to become a teacher, but her real dream was to be a lawyer. The dream would have to wait, however, until she could save up some money for tuition. She taught at a small rural school in Alabama for a while then returned to Nashville for a research job. The following year she taught classes in Mississippi and then in Georgia before moving back to Montgomery in 1938 to help out at her dad's new store. It was there she met Henry Dickerson, a handsome young hotel worker with a reputation as a womanizer. The two fell in love, and only six weeks later, on October 5, 1938, they were married. Ten months later, Mahala gave birth to triplet boys.

The Dickerson triplets at about age six. Left to right: Henri Christophe (Chris), John Adair, and Alfred Dungee —Courtesy John A. Dickerson

The babies—Alfred Dungee, John Adair, and Henri Christophe (Chris) Dickerson—arrived on August 25, 1939. Shortly after they were born, Mahala and Henry divorced, and Henry moved to Cleveland, Ohio, and became a banker. Now a single parent, Mahala took an office job at a Catholic mission in Montgomery. Later she returned to teaching school and sold cosmetics as a sideline. When the United States entered World War II, she found a better-paying job at nearby Tuskegee Army Airfield, a training facility for African American pilots.

After about a year and a half at the army base, Mahala took a research position at Tuskegee Institute, a well-known Negro college founded by George Washington Carver in 1881. A year later, in 1944, the project Mahala was working on was moved to Howard University, the highly respected African American institution in Washington, D.C. Leaving the boys, now six years old, with her parents, Mahala moved to Washington. In the fall of 1945, she received a scholarship to attend the Howard University School of Law. It was the fulfillment of her lifelong dream.

As always, Mahala studied hard and earned good grades. She also joined the Alpha Kappa Alpha sorority and enjoyed many college activities. But she missed her sons dreadfully, racking up high telephone bills and riding the segregated train to Montgomery to visit them whenever she could. Finally, in June 1948, she received the law degree she had worked so hard for, again graduating cum laude. She returned to Alabama to take the state bar examination, but being black and female, she had difficulty finding the five sponsors she needed to join the Alabama Bar Association. She was finally successful, becoming the first African American woman to be admitted. Shortly afterward, she joined the National Bar Association, a nationwide organization for African American lawyers. In those days, the primary national attorney group, the American Bar Association, restricted its membership to whites.

In the fall, Mahala went back to Washington to work for the federal government for another six months before returning to Montgomery, reuniting with her boys at last. She opened her first law office in Montgomery in July 1949, and her practice was an immediate success. But four months later, on November 11, 1949, Mahala's beloved father, John Ashley, suddenly died of a heart attack. Feeling that "something deep and lasting had vanished from my life," she found solace in hard work.

In 1950 Mahala enrolled for a summer session at Pendle Hill, a Quaker study center near Philadelphia, Pennsylvania, to help her heal her grief as well as to hone personal and professional discipline. Mahala had been raised a Baptist, but she had attended some Quaker (Friends) meetings while she was in law school in Washington and was attracted to the church's values of pacifism, social service, and human equality. Mahala said she had become a pacifist while working at the air base during the war, having met many young pilots who were later killed. Pendle Hill's peaceful woodland setting and supportive community was just what she needed; she later described that summer as one of the most inspiring experiences of her life. She also noted that it was at Pendle Hill that she first learned to swim, an activity she pursued vigorously for the rest of her life.

Upon returning from her retreat, Mahala opened a second law office in Tuskegee. Later she traveled to Nashville to attend the annual meeting of the National Bar Association, where she met fellow attorney Frank Beckwith. Even though Frank lived in Indianapolis, Indiana, the two began dating. Thinking that "the creation of a family with two parents would give my children greater stability as well as bring me more happiness," Mahala agreed to marry Frank and move to Indiana. They wed in May 1951.

Upon moving to Indianapolis with the triplets, now twelve years old, Mahala took the Indiana bar exam, and in 1952 she became the second black woman member of the Indiana Bar Association. She joined her new husband in his law practice and settled into the community. Mahala was happy for a time. She liked Indiana. Although the state had outlawed most segregation, many public schools had not yet integrated their students. After some assertive words and actions, Mahala and Frank enrolled the boys in a nearby junior high school that had previously been all white.

Frank often teased Mahala about her willingness to take cases for little or no payment. He predicted that she would "die young and die poor because you put a thousand dollars' worth of work into a ten-dollar case." Her response was "Even if I die poor, I will always feel that my life has been rich because of my many friends."

Sadly, like Mahala's first marriage, her marriage to Frank ended in divorce. She never married again. Frank Beckwith later became a judge and a civil-rights advocate; in 1960, he ran for U.S. president in the Republican primary, becoming the first African American to seek the presidential nomination of a major party.

After the divorce, Mahala remained in Indiana while the boys went out of state to attend high school. The triplets ended up graduating from different high schools in different states. In the summer of 1958, with her boys on their own, Mahala took her fateful vacation trip to Alaska and decided to live there, not only for its natural beauty but also for its relatively progressive policies—the territory had enacted an antidiscrimination law back in 1945 (see previous chapter on Elizabeth Peratrovich). Mahala also saw a need for better legal representation among the territory's poor and underprivileged, whom she hoped to serve.

Even in the far north and despite the laws, prejudice and discrimination were far from extinct. The Native Alaskans had been fighting for their rights for years, with mixed success. Although there were very few African Americans in the territory at that time, the ones who lived there, Mahala soon found out, often faced the same unfair treatment as that found in the Lower Forty-eight. The day after her arrival in Anchorage, when she went to the land office to apply for a homestead, she was told there were none in the area. The nearest available plot was in Homer, nearly three hundred miles away, the clerk said.

Mahala was about to leave in disappointment when a bystander—a white man with a southern accent—intervened. "Why don't you show her the ones in Wasilla that you just showed me?" he said. The clerk turned red and huffily pulled out a map of the area, threw it on the desk, and walked away. The man opened the map and pointed to a site. "Here's one with a lake on it," he said. It was a 160-acre tract less than an hour's drive from Anchorage. Mahala was sold.

The man left, and Mahala never saw him again. Some of her friends later joked that maybe he was an angel. When the clerk came back, Mahala said she wanted the homestead the man had shown her on the map. The clerk told her that homesteaders had to go out to see a property before they could sign on it. Mahala left, but she suspected the clerk was lying to her again. That evening, she read up on the Homestead Act and its requirements. Sure enough, there was no rule about seeing the land before buying it. The next morning she marched back to the land office and signed the forms for the homestead she wanted, sight unseen, making Mahala Dickerson the first black homesteader in the Mat-Su Valley.

In order to practice law in her new homeland, Mahala needed to join the bar association in Alaska. Although she did not experience as much difficulty in being admitted to the bar in Alaska as she had in Alabama, it took her nearly a year to receive her license. In 1959, the year Alaska became a state, Mahala became the first African American of either sex to join the Alaska Bar. Upon her acceptance into the Alaska Bar, the previously all-white American Bar Association then admitted her, she said, "without comment."

Mahala still needed an office in Anchorage where she could open her practice. She searched the local newspaper ads for a place to rent but found much of the same housing discrimination she had faced in the South. Finally a white man who opposed racism agreed to rent her an office and help her get set up.

From the first day of her practice, Mahala did not lack clients. Some were minorities, and many were poor. She sometimes accepted payments other than cash for her services, or even none at all. It was not long before the "black woman lawyer" was known throughout the valley for her altruism as well as her fearlessness in fighting injustice. It was an exciting and happy start in her new home state. Mahala's happiness would not last long, however; little did she know, tragedy was waiting just around the corner.

In June 1960, two of Mahala's sons, John and Alfred, came to visit her and see her homestead, on which she had just finished building her cabin. Since graduating from high school, John had been attending the University of Utah, while Chris was studying at the American Academy of Dramatic Arts in New York City, and Alfred was living in Los Angeles, where he planned to enroll at UCLA in the fall. Only three days after their arrival, on June 22, Alfred, age twenty, drowned in a nearby lake. "I had suffered from the pains of death before," Mahala wrote. "But losing a child was a much deeper hurt. This was a pain the like of which only another mother can understand. I lost my son, Alfred, my firstborn."

Mahala dedicated a portion of her homestead as the Alfred D. Dickerson Memorial Cemetery, where she buried Alfred and reserved a plot for herself and her other two sons. Some of the land was reserved for the local Quakers, who eventually built a Friends Meeting House there. Mahala often invited the Friends into her home, where they were welcome to use her heated indoor swimming pool or to ice skate on her lake in the winter. Quakers from as far away as Fairbanks visited Mahala's homestead and enjoyed her hospitality. Also in memory of Alfred, Mahala founded Al-Acres, a charitable, educational, and religious organization that gave scholarships and awards to deserving black students.

After Alfred died, Mahala's other two sons, John and Chris, established lives of their own. John became a physical therapist, working in private practice and onboard cruise liners. He lived in New York City for some years before returning to Alaska, where he now lives at his mother's homestead. Chris, who had been a talented performer in high school theatrical and musical productions, went to New York City after graduating high school to study acting, singing, and dance at the American Academy of Dramatic Arts. To strengthen his vocal chords for singing, he started training with weights in the early 1960s. He later moved to Los Angeles, and within a few years he was participating in body-building competitions, winning numerous contests around the country.

In 1970 Chris Dickerson became the first African American to win the Amateur Athletic Union's title of Mr. America. Among the many other state, national, and international competitions Chris won were the National Amateur Body Builders Association's Mr. Universe title in 1973 and 1974 and the International Federation of Bodybuilding (IFBB) title of Mr. Olympia in 1982. After retiring from bodybuilding in 1994, Chris settled in Florida. He was inducted into the IFBB Hall of Fame in 2000 and received the Ben Weider Lifetime Achievement Award in 2008.

Remaining in Wasilla, Mahala loved her homestead and the rural Alaska lifestyle, even though the weather was unpredictable, the roads were primitive, and services were scarce. She remembered how the homesteaders in her area helped one another when someone got stuck in the mud or snow. Those with no water or phone service were welcome to use their neighbor's. Mahala deeply appreciated the homesteaders' community spirit and commitment to helping others, and she jumped right in to do her part. She often invited her neighbors to her home to discuss problems they had in common or just to be social. Since the road she lived on had no school bus service, Mahala frequently picked up kids on her way into town and gave them a ride to school. She even held an annual Easter egg hunt for the local children.

On Friday, March 27, 1964, a serious crisis brought everyone in Anchorage together. Around 5:30 p.m., a major earthquake erupted in south-central Alaska. Within a few minutes, much of downtown

Anchorage was leveled, and dozens of homes were disabled, damaged, or destroyed. In the chaos that followed, people who still had heat and water invited their less fortuate neighbors to share their homes.

Mahala was in her office downtown when the tremors hit. Her building sustained some minor damage, but she and her staff were unharmed. Some friends took her in until the roads were cleared for her to get home. Out in Wasilla, Mahala's homestead and those of her neighbors, luckily, had escaped the worst of the quake and suffered little property damage and few injuries. Many Alaskans, however, were not so lucky—about seventy-five homes in Anchorage were lost, and some of Alaska's coastal areas saw massive destruction from the subsequent tsumanis. In the end, about 130 Alaskans lost their lives in the disaster.

As the years went by, Mahala's practice grew, and she was winning wide recognition as an advocate for workers' rights. She argued many cases involving racial and gender discrimination, and she did not hesitate to fight big corporations, the Anchorage Police Department, the Alaska Bar Association, or even the federal government. One friend and fellow attorney, Rex Butler, remembered being told by another lawyer upon his arrival in Alaska, "Rex, you see those mountains out there? Those mountains are littered with the bones of lawyers who underestimated M. Ashley Dickerson."

Some of Mahala's cases set precedents. She wrote, "I found that so many of my cases, which later turned out to be landmark cases, came to me because I was the only attorney who had the guts to take them, or was naive enough to take them. It did not concern me at all . . . to take up the cause of a person discriminated against because of age, race, or physical condition."

In one well-publicized case in 1975, Mahala represented a female professor at the University of Alaska Anchorage (UAA) whose salary was considerably less than that of her male colleague who did the same work. It was one of the first such cases ever brought to court. Arguing for equal pay regardless of sex, Mahala lost the case, but it was appealed, and the higher court reversed the decision. Despite the university's loss in that case, in 1994 UAA granted Mahala an honorary doctorate of law degree for her advocacy of minority rights. Given that she had sued that very school nineteen years earlier, the award had extra meaning for her.

Mahala Dickerson in her later years —Rubenstein Library and University Archives, Duke University

During the 1980s, the accolades began to pour in for Mahala. In 1982 she received the Freedom Award from the NAACP (National Association for the Advancement of Colored People). The following year, she became the first African American president of the National Association of Women Lawyers, a position she held for two years. In 1985 she was honored with two major awards—she won the Zeta Phi Beta Woman of the Year Award for distinguished service in the field of law, and the National Spirit of Assembly Baha'i of Alaska presented her with their annual Honor Kempton Service to Humanity Award. The 1980s brought sad news as well, when Mahala's beloved older sister, Erna, died in 1984.

Also in the mid-1980s, Mahala teamed up with a partner, Johnny O. Gibbons, and opened the Dickerson & Gibbons law firm in Anchorage. Mahala and Johnny remained partners until Mahala stopped practicing at age ninety-one. In 1984, when she was seventy-one, Mahala was asked by the *Anchorage Daily News* why she was still working twelve-hour days. "Whenever there's somebody being mistreated, if they want me, I'll help them," she said. "I'm just not afraid to fight somebody big."

The 1990s brought both bad and good to Mahala's life. In January 1991, Mahala was quietly reading in her homestead cabin when she noticed flames from her fireplace had expanded into the room. She ran into the yard and helplessly watched her dream house burn to the ground. It was a painful loss, but she rebuilt quickly. Showing her typical optimistic spirit, Mahala wrote, "My burned house has been replaced by a more beautiful one." Later that year another tragedy struck when her cherished little sister, Harriet, preceded Mahala in death.

In 1995 Mahala received one of her best-known honors when the National Bar Association presented her with the Margaret Brent Award, established to recognize female lawyers who have excelled in their field and have paved the way for others. This prestigious award had previously gone to such prominent women as Ruth Bader Ginsburg, Sandra Day O'Connor, Anita Hill, and Hillary Rodham Clinton. Mahala was also inducted into the National Bar Association's Hall of Fame in 1999.

Mahala was often asked how she managed to succeed in spite of having "two strikes against" her, being black and being female. "Those things are both in my favor," she maintained. "Being black gives me a certain ability to empathize with the oppressed and mistreated; being female gives me a certain insight into human problems, which no male could ever have. . . . I have felt, throughout the years, that clients of all races, ages, and creeds have been more at ease with me *because* I was black and female."

After working for years on her autobiography, entitled *Delayed Justice for Sale*, Mahala finally published it in 1998. She said that she chose the title to reflect her hope that those who have suffered injustices will live long enough to see them corrected, just as she had. In the book she describes not only her personal struggles but also many of the cases she took on, some of which she won and some she did not. "To me all of these people, black or white, male or female, were seeking their freedom, and freedom from discrimination was merely one of those freedoms. Freedom to earn a living, freedom to receive equal pay, freedom from taking of property by the state without due process of law, freedom from police brutality—all were included in our Constitution and [are] inherent in being an American."

On October 15, 2002, a resolution by the city of Anchorage recognized and honored Mahala for her "Lifetime Commitment to Equality and Justice." At the time, at age ninety, she was the oldest practicing attorney in the state. She left active practice the following year. In 2006, Mahala was once again honored for her invaluable contributions, this time in the state of her birth, winning the Alabama State Bar Association's Maud McLure Kelly Award, presented yearly to an outstanding female lawyer.

Mahala died in Wasilla on February 19, 2007. She was ninety-four. Major newspapers around Alaska and the nation carried the news of Mahala Dickerson's death, and Alaska's governor ordered state flags to be lowered to half-mast in her honor. Mahala was buried next to her son Alfred on her Wasilla homestead.

Upon hearing of her death, an Alaska Friends member said that the finest gift Mahala left was her example: "pragmatism lightened with humor, . . . weathering disappointment and tragedy with grace, . . . an undiminished capacity for joy, . . . and the desire and ability to set things right when she saw injustice."

In 2009, two years after her death, Mahala was inducted into the Alaska Women's Hall of Fame. Later, Knik Elementary School in Wasilla named its library for her. A collection of Mahala's papers is archived at Duke University's rare book and manuscript library.

As one radio broadcast summed up Mahala's life in a "Women in History" profile in 1997, "Throughout her fifty-year career, Dickerson fought in court as she did in life and won landmark cases for civil rights and against discrimination and prejudice. . . . Mahala Ashley Dickerson, an Alaskan pioneer."

CELIA HUNTER AND GINNY HILL WOOD

"Alaskans Organize"

At the turn of the nineteenth century, Alaska's wealth was in sea otter skins. At the turn of the twentieth, it was in gold. But for Celia Hunter and Ginny Wood, in the second half of the twentieth century, Alaska's wealth was in its wilderness, whose treasures they worked to see protected and shared with all Americans.

Celia and Ginny had similar backgrounds—both were from Washington state, both were trained airplane pilots, and both had served as WASPs (Women Airforce Service Pilots) during World War II. After they met, became friends, and flew to Alaska together, both fell in love with the territory and its wild places. From there, they would team up, first as business partners, then as environmental activists, and together make history.

Celia Hunter had not set out to be an environmentalist—a word few people had ever even heard at the time she was born in 1919. She hadn't expected to devote most of her adult life to conserving Alaska's wilderness; she never even thought she would ever live in Alaska. As she said many years later, "These things just happened."

Born on January 13, 1919, on a small farm in the logging town of Arlington, Washington, Celia Margaret Hunter was the eldest of

Celia Hunter,
circa 1926,
with brothers
Russ and
Glen —Courtesy
Jenna Hertz,
Flickr Creative

four children born to Ira and Bessie Ashmun Hunter, both Quakers. Celia had two brothers, Glen and Russ, and a sister, Charlotte, the youngest, born nine years after Celia. The Hunter children grew up in the Marysville area, north of Seattle, during the Great Depression of the 1930s. Their mother had been a schoolteacher, from whom Celia inherited her love of books. Their father was a logger-turned-farmer, though Celia described him as a jack-of-all-trades. The family was poor but loving.

After Celia graduated from Marysville High School in 1936, she attended business college for a semester then took a job as an accounts clerk at a timber company in nearby Everett, Washington. Each day on her way to work, she passed Everett Airport. As an admirer of Amelia Earhart and Charles Lindbergh—two aviation heroes of the 1920s and '30s—Celia was drawn to the idea of becoming a pilot, and she decided to sign up for lessons as soon as she turned twenty-one.

In the fall of 1939, Celia enrolled at Linfield College. At the time, a brand-new federal program, the Civilian Pilot Training Program (CPTP), was offering flight training to college students. Although the United States had not yet entered the European war that would soon become known as World War II, the government understood that American involvement was likely on the horizon, and the nation would need pilots to support the war effort at home and abroad.

In January of 1940, a few days after her twenty-first birthday, Celia signed up for the CPTP. By April she had taken her first solo flight. When she earned her private pilot's license in 1941, her mother was her first passenger. Within a few years, Celia would meet Ginny Hill (later Ginny Wood), launching a lifelong friendship and partnership.

Virginia (Ginny) Hill was born in Moro, Oregon, on October 24, 1917, and grew up in Waterville, Washington, in the central part of the state. Her parents were Charles Edwin (Ed) and Edythe Brunquist Hill, both of Massachusetts. Ginny had one sister, Marjorie, who was three years younger.

Ed Hill was an agricultural engineer and an avid outdoorsman. Taking after her father, Ginny loved adventure and the outdoors. Growing up, she skiied, hiked, rafted, and rode horses. As a teenager, she even guided horseback trips through Washington's natural areas.

Like Celia, Ginny was captivated by the exploits of Amelia Earhart and Charles Lindbergh, but unlike her future partner, she knew she wanted to fly from an early age. She had her first plane ride at age four, sitting on her father's lap next to the pilot, a barnstormer (stunt flyer). By the time she was school age, Ginny's goal was set.

After high school, in 1936, Ginny enrolled at the University of Washington in Seattle. She completed her first year, then took a year off from school to tour Europe. When she returned to the university, she heard about the Civilian Pilot Training Program, which

Ginny Hill and her sister Margie, 1923 —Courtesy Jenna Hertz, Flickr Creative Commons

would be opening enrollment in January 1939. Twenty-one-year-old Ginny was among the first to sign up. By 1942 she had earned both a commercial pilot license and a flight instructor rating.

By 1943, World War II was well under way. Independently, Celia and Ginny learned of a new Air Force program that trained women to fly small planes for the military. The two immediately applied for the program, which would train them to become Women Air Force Service Pilots (WASPs). Both were accepted into the program and both passed their training with flying colors. As WASPs, or "Flyer Girls," Celia and Ginny flew sophisticated fighter aircraft, shuttling the planes from the factories where they were built to Air Force training centers or wherever they were needed within the forty-eight states. "We never knew where we'd be assigned from day to day," Ginny later recalled.

Ginny Hill poses with military planes, 1944
—Courtesy Jenna Hertz, Flickr Creative Commons

Celia Hunter in the cockpit of a P-47 Thunderbolt, 1944
—Courtesy Jenna Hertz, Flickr Creative Commons

The WASPs learned to fly the "hottest" planes of the day, fighters and bombers with names like Mustangs, Cobras, Lightnings, Thunderbolts, and Black Widows. In spite of the flyer girls' skill, Air Force regulations prevented females not only from flying on combat missions but also from piloting war planes outside the States. During the war, many military planes were flown to Alaska to be transferred to the Soviet Union (by that point our allies in the war), but the WASPs could take the planes only as far as Great Falls, Montana, where male pilots picked them up and flew them to Fairbanks. The WASPs were told there were "no facilities" for women in Alaska. This ban only served to pique the curiousity of Celia Hunter and Ginny Wood. As the male pilots returned from the territory with stories of glorious landscapes and wild weather, each of these two adventurers grew determined to get there on her own.

During the war, Ginny and Celia had a mutual friend, B.J. Erickson, who had introduced them, and they had occasionally run into each other at various landing spots, but it was not until later that they became friends. After the WASPs were disbanded in December of 1944, toward the end of the war, both women moved to Seattle, where Celia enrolled for classes at the University of Washington and Ginny took a job as a flight instructor.

In the spring of 1945, B.J. Erickson called Ginny to tell her about a job opening near Portland, Oregon. The employer, a plane-refurbishing company called Reconstruction Finance Corporation, was looking for pilots to pick up old planes from around the country and fly them back to Portland for repairs and restoration. Would she be interested in the job? Eager to return to piloting, Ginny said yes. The company needed several pilots, B.J. added. She suggested Ginny call Celia Hunter. She did, and the two of them left that night for Portland. Ginny and Celia, often flying in tandem, enjoyed the job and became close friends. In the fall, Ginny returned to Seattle and resumed giving flying lessons, and Celia went back to Everett, where she, too, worked as a flight instructor.

The following spring, in 1946, Ginny invited Celia on a ski trip to Mount Baker, in Washington's Cascade Range, where she was renting a cabin. Celia, who had never been on skis before, was reluctant, but her friend persuaded her to come, offering to teach her how to ski. And so the two spent several happy weeks exploring the Mount Baker area and cementing their friendship. That summer, Ginny invited Celia to come sailing with her and a friend named Isabelle "Pete" Madison. They three women spent the next four months on Ginny's sailboat, exploring the inlets and ports of the Pacific coast up to Victoria Island in British Columbia, Canada. Ginny had hoped to sail all the way to Alaska, but the adventurers were not able to make it that far. In September, Ginny and Celia went back to their respective jobs as flight instructors.

About two months later, in November of 1946, Celia called Ginny telling her of an opportunity to finally see Alaska. An Alaska pilot and businessman named Gene Jack, Celia said, was looking for pilots to take the war-surplus planes he had just purchased in Seattle and deliver them to Weeks Field in Fairbanks. Naturally, Ginny jumped at the chance. The women would be flying in tandem during the trip, which was expected to take a few days. They estimated that they'd be in the air for about thirty hours in total.

When Celia and Ginny met Gene Jack, he hired them immediately and showed them the planes. One was a seven-seat Stinson Gullwing, which Celia would fly, and Ginny would pilot a two-seat Stinson L-5 Sentinel spotter plane, which was barely airworthy and had no heater. The friends would nickname that one "Li'l Igloo."

After a few weeks preparing the planes and waiting for the weather to clear, the two women left Seattle on December 6, 1946. The radio in one plane couldn't transmit signals, and the one in the other couldn't receive them, so Celia and Ginny relied on hand signals to relay radio transmissions back and forth. Due to terrible weather, the trip ended up taking them not thirty hours but twenty-seven days, out of which they were able to fly only four days. To find their way, they basically followed the route of the newly built Alcan Highway. Since airfields were few in the Yukon, Celia and Ginny sometimes used the highway itself as a landing strip. When they stopped, they often had to set fire pots under their engines to keep them warm. On one leg of the trip, Ginny's L'il Igloo was so frigid that Celia had to "chip her out" of the cockpit when they landed. "She was so cold she couldn't move," Celia recalled.

Celia and Ginny finally reached Fairbanks on New Year's Day, 1947. A blizzard was blowing so badly that they had trouble finding the tiny landing strip at Weeks Field, but both landed safely. The temperature in Fairbanks that day was about fifty degrees below zero.

Celia and Ginny had no plans to stay in Alaska, but the severe snowstorms had grounded all commercial flights, so they could not get back to Seattle until the weather improved. In the meantime, Gene Jack, now back in Fairbanks, offered to pay the two women to haul cargo to his store in Kotzebue. During the trip, the women were weathered-in several times at various Eskimo villages, where they got to know some of the Alaska Natives.

Back in Fairbanks, Ginny and Celia decided to try out a local ski run at the nearby army base. It was while skiing that Ginny met Morton "Woody" Wood, a Maine native and war veteran who was taking classes at the University of Alaska in Fairbanks. The two began dating. "Oh boy, was he a good dancer!" Ginny recalled. The relationship was not very serious, however. Neither Woody nor Ginny planned to stay in Alaska for long.

By late February, Celia and Ginny "decided that we might as well stick around and see what the summer was like" in Fairbanks. They found jobs at Charles (Chuck) West's Arctic Alaska Travel Service (later called Westours), Fairbanks's first aerial tourist service. The women decided to stay in Alaska for the summer and work for West, running the office, planning local car tours of Fairbanks, and later piloting the first-ever tourist flights to Kotzebue and Nome.

Ginny and Celia left at the end of the summer of 1947. Their eight months in Alaska had been exciting, but the two had already enrolled, through an Air Force–sponsored program, for fall classes at the University of Stockholm, so off they went for a semester of study in Sweden. When classes ended, the two skied in Austria for a few weeks, then bicycled through war-torn Europe for ten months. In defeated Germany, they saw "acre after acre of blasted, shattered dwellings and buildings."

In the meantime, Woody had gone to France to attend college for a year. In October 1948 he met up with Ginny and Celia in Paris.

Celia (left) and Ginny on their bicycle tour of Europe, 1948
—Courtesy Jenna Hertz, Flickr Creative Commons

During the week they spent together in Paris, the spark between Ginny and Woody reignited. But both were involved in their own busy lives—in fact, Woody had a girlfriend back home—so they kept things casual. Woody spent another week with Ginny, Celia, and some friends hiking in Switzerland before returning to school. After that, Ginny and Celia were ready to go home. They returned to the States in December 1948 by hitching a ride on a tanker ship. Upon arriving in New York, Ginny bought an old Jeep and the pair drove back to Seattle.

Back home, Ginny and Celia came to feel that life in the United States was too complicated and materialistic. After touring the devastation in Europe, Americans seemed complacent and overly affluent by comparison. The women began to miss the simpler way of life that Alaska offered, although they still had no intention of living there permanently. In the fall of 1949 Ginny and Celia headed north again with a plan to finance a winter of skiing in the States. They went to Kotzebue, bought up a large supply of mukluks (Eskimo boots), and returned to the States to sell them to various ski resorts on the West Coast. When they had sold everything, they decided to take Ginny's Jeep to Mexico.

On the way south, Ginny and Celia stopped in California to visit with their friend Woody Woods, who was at that point enrolled at the University of California at Berkeley. While in California, Ginny was surprised when Woody suddenly asked her to marry him. They were married in Seattle the following summer, on July 20, 1950.

In the fall, the newlyweds returned to Berkeley for Woody to finish his forestry degree at the university. He also wanted to learn to fly a plane like his bride, so Ginny gave him lessons. When Woody earned his pilot's license, the Woods bought a small plane of their own.

Woody was in his final semester at Berkeley when he received a job offer to be a ranger at Mount McKinley National Park (now called Denali National Park and Preserve). Both he and Ginny had tired of city life. "Want to go back to Alaska?" Woody asked his wife. "I sure would!" she replied. The very day Woody graduated, they loaded up their plane and flew north.

When the Woods arrived in Fairbanks in June 1951, the Park Service informed Woody that he'd be working not at McKinley, but at the remote Katmai National Park, in southwestern Alaska, for the summer. He and Ginny were disappointed, but they enjoyed exploring the isolated area for potential recreational development. In the meantime, Celia had moved back to Alaska herself, resuming her work for Chuck West in Fairbanks.

Shortly after the Woods' arrival, Celia shared with them an idea to open a rustic camp in McKinley Park, which at the time had no accommodations other than a large, fancy hotel. The resort Celia had in mind was much different. Inspired by the hut system she and Ginny had seen in Europe, where hikers and skiers traveling through the mountains could spend the night in primitive huts that had been built along backcountry trails, Celia conceived of a basic camp for visitors to explore Alaska's natural wonders while making a minimal impact on the environment—what is known today as "leaving a small footprint." They would build a log lodge and a few simple cabins, and from there, their guests could freely explore Alaska's magnificent backcountry. It would be the first Alaska business based on what is now called ecotourism.

Woody and Ginny loved the idea, and the three decided to give it a try. They pooled their money, and while the Woods were in Katmai, Celia began looking for an appropriate site near Mount McKinley (Denali) on which to establish their retreat. Later that summer, she called the Woods to come out and see a place she'd found. They did, and all three agreed that it was exactly what they were looking for: sixty-seven acres at the western boundary of Mount McKinley National Park, with a small pond, a rocky ridge, and a "Wow!" view of Denali. Celia filed a Homestead Act claim on the property.

When Ginny and Woody returned to Fairbanks in the fall of 1951, Woody began his ranger job at Mount McKinley. He and Ginny spent the fall and winter in a log cabin inside the park, traveling around by dogsled. In the spring, the Park Service told Woody he was going to be transferred to California's Yosemite National Park. But by then, Woody was in love with Denali. He quit. Then he, Ginny, and Celia began working on the camp in earnest. Beginning with two tent shelters, they subsequently constructed a number of rustic cabins with spruce logs they harvested on their land, supplemented by reclaimed materials from the neighboring Park Service. Friends and visitors who stopped by to have a look often stuck around to help the partners clear the road, haul logs, and build structures.

Camp Denali opened for business in June 1952. Each small cabin had simple furniture and a wood stove, but no plumbing, electricity, or phone service. Behind the cabins stood several detached outhouses and an outdoor water spigot. Each cabin also had a clear view of Denali, the tallest mountain in North America, locally known as the "Great One."

Camp Denali's owners didn't need to advertise. Word of mouth kept them supplied with guests. Wanting to keep the camp small so it wouldn't endanger the very wilderness feel they were working to preserve, the partners stopped adding cabins when they had seventeen.

At first, the owners had not planned to provide food for their guests, but when the camp's first visitors started trickling in, few brought their own provisions, so the owners began making simple, wholesome meals part of the package. Eventually, Camp Denali also started offering special programs in backcountry hiking, wildlife photography, ecology, and other topics of interest to guests. Some visitors preferred no program at all, just the opportunity to experience the wilderness around them.

On porch of lodge at Camp Denali, circa 1959. Left to right: Celia Hunter, Romany Wood (on Celia's lap), Ginny Wood, Woody Wood
—Courtesy Jenna Hertz, Flickr Creative Commons

After their first summer at Camp Denali, the Woods bought some land outside Fairbanks, in a neighborhood affectionately known as Dogpatch, where they and Celia built simple log cabins to serve as their home base during the winter off-season. Later, the Woods expanded their home. In May 1956, Ginny and Woody welcomed daughter Romany, their only child. The Woods would divorce in 1960, after ten years of marriage. The following year, Woody moved permanently to Seattle. After the divorce, Ginny continued to operate Camp Denali with Celia.

Running Camp Denali kept Celia and Ginny busy during the summer, but in the winter months they became more and more involved in political issues. It was in Ginny's Dogpatch cabin that she and Celia would organize the Alaska Conservation Society (ACS), the first environmental group in the state, in 1959, shortly after Alaska was granted statehood. The organization, which became official in 1960, included a large number of scientists, who helped compile scientific data to present to officials and the public. "We could go to a hearing and wow them because we got our facts straight," Ginny said.

The ACS was formed, in part, to support the efforts of veteran conservationists Olaus and Margaret (Mardy) Murie to pass a federal law protecting a large section of the Arctic ecosystem from development. Olaus, a wildlife biologist, and wife Mardy were both leading members of the Wilderness Society, founded in 1935. Celia and Ginny had become good friends with the couple after the Muries' trip to Alaska in 1956. The ACS joined forces with the Muries and the Wilderness Society to lobby for creation of the Arctic National Wildlife Range (ANWR), which would include almost 9 million acres of mountains and coastal plain in far-northeastern Alaska. In addition to its Dall sheep, grizzly bears, and myriad other fauna, the area was the wintering ground for the Porcupine herd of caribou, which numbered more than 100,000.

Unlike the nationwide Wilderness Society, ACS membership was restricted to Alaska residents; Celia and Ginny felt a group of Alaskans would get more support from fellow Alaskans, especially the Alaska legislators in Congress, than would any groups from outside. The society's first newletter was emblazoned with the motto "Alaskans Organize." Indeed, the ACS found backing not only from concerned Alaska residents but also from Northland businesses such as wilderness-tour companies, outdoor-gear shops, and others that would benefit from the law's establishment. However, the organizers were finding it difficult to garner support in Washington, D.C.

Both Celia and Ginny testified before Congressional committees. In her appearance before the Committee on Interstate and Foreign Commerce in 1959, Celia showed that mining was no longer in second place (after the military) for generating revenue for the state. It was now tourism. She emphasized the importance to the tourist industry of safeguarding such resources as pure air, clean rivers, and thriving wildlife. Ginny also testified in 1959, saying, "The esthetic, spiritual, recreational, and educational values of such an area are those one cannot put a price tag on, any more than one can on a sunset, a piece of poetry, a symphony, or a friendship."

In spite of opposition from pro-development groups and individuals, support for the ANWR grew statewide and nationally. Finally, on December 7, 1960, in the last days of President Dwight Eisenhower's administration, the president issued a proclamation establishing the Arctic National Wildlife Range (later called the Arctic National Wildlife Refuge). Olaus and Mardy Murie hugged each other and wept happy tears, and Celia and Ginny were "giddy with joy."

Even in the midst of celebrating this historic victory, Celia, Ginny, and the ACS were already in the throes of fighting two more pressing threats to Alaska's environment. One was a federal proposal called Project Chariot; the other was the proposed Rampart Dam project.

Project Chariot was an Atomic Energy Commission (AEC) plan to use nuclear bombs to blast out a new harbor at Point Hope, on the Arctic Ocean in northwestern Alaska. The nuclear-power promoters of the AEC wanted to test the possible economic benefits of nuclear power in the Northland. They also claimed that the new port would benefit residents by providing easier shipping access in the region. While Alaska's congressional delegation and business organizations throughout the state approved of the project, introduced in 1958, opponents noted that the commission had failed to study the potential long-term effects of radiation on the local Natives, on caribou and other wildlife, and on the land itself.

Outraged by the AEC's plan, Celia and Ginny began running the mimeograph machine (an early type of copier) at Dogpatch almost nonstop. They sent a thousand copies of their thirty-page newsletter, which presented facts and opinions from numerous Alaska scientists, to government officials in Washington, D.C., and to conservationists throughout the nation. One of its recipients, Secretary of the Interior Stewart Udall, realized that the AEC had never consulted his office about the project, igniting his skepticism.

As word spread and conservationist groups around the nation joined the cause, public pressure to study the environmental impact of Project Chariot mounted. "They thought they could push everybody around," Celia said, "and they suddenly discovered they were up against an informed citizenry." The AEC was forced to conduct a series of studies, producing what was probably the first-ever Environmental Impact Statement.

Tracing the food chain in the fragile Arctic, researchers determined that contaminated lichen could affect the caribou that fed on it, in turn affecting the Inupiaq Eskimos who ate the caribou meat. To add any more radioactivity in the Arctic would likely be disastrous, the study concluded. The impact statement, Celia said later, "really pulled the [rug] out from under the project." In 1962, though it was never officially cancelled, Project Chariot was put on hold indefinitely. The AEC had been stopped, as one writer noted, by "a relative handful of committed people, a small Eskimo village, whale hunters and bureaucrats, bush pilots and church ladies, [and] log-cabin conservationists" such as Celia and Ginny.

The Alaska Conservation Society's next battle—stopping yet another federal proposal—would prove even more challenging. The Army Corps of Engineers had first proposed building a hydroelectric dam at the town of Rampart, in the Yukon Flats northwest of Fairbanks, in 1954. The territory was growing rapidly and would need electrical power to keep up with the increasing demand. The

Corps' proposed dam would create Alaska's largest hydroelectric plant. In addition, damming the Yukon River would form a three-hundred-mile-long reservoir—an area larger than Lake Erie.

The Yukon Flats were made up mostly of wetlands and served as the breeding grounds for millions of waterfowl. Conservationists recognized that the dam would not only destroy this wildlife habitat, it would also flood several villages of the Athabaskan Indians, among them the historic community of Rampart itself. Yet advocates insisted that the harm would be negligible and that the state needed the power.

A few months after Alaska became a state in 1959, Alaska's Senator Ernest Gruening, who supported the dam proposal, passed a resolution calling for an official feasibility study of the Rampart site. This and subsequent studies would take place over the next several years. Even as the studies were under way, Celia, Ginny, and the ACS were already hard at work to show that the project would be a serious assault on the environment.

Celia and Ginny were not alone in their objections to the dam. Native Alaskans joined in the debates at the prospect of losing their villages. Other groups pointed out the project's cost and the limited market for the power. Environmentalists protested against the loss of wetlands so critical for waterfowl.

Early government studies determined that the dam was economically feasible and would attract new industry to Alaska, but a later report by the U.S. Fish and Wildlife Service, released in April 1964, denounced the project on environmental grounds. Two months later, the results of a Natural Resource Council study reached a conclusion similar to that of the USFWS.

In the meantime, the ACS labored tirelessly to raise public awareness of the damage that would result if the dam were built. Finally, in 1967, the U.S. Secretary of the Interior, Stewart Udall, rejected the Rampart Dam proposal. Thirteen years later, as a result of continued pressure from conservationists, President Jimmy Carter created the Yukon Flats National Wildlife Sanctuary, shielding the region from further development.

In addition to the Project Chariot and Rampart Dam protests, Celia and Ginny worked on local issues throughout the state. They used their influence to protect wolves—calling for the removal of bounties that hunters received for shooting the animals—and helped organize residents of communities statewide to build trails, preserve open spaces, and study environmental problems.

In 1964 Celia earned her bachelor's degree in botany from the University of Alaska in Fairbanks. That same year, President Lyndon Johnson signed into law the Wilderness Act, which protected millions of new acres from development. It was a piece of legislation that the Wilderness Society, including her friends the Muries, had spent eight years lobbying for. Five years later, the Wilderness Society, impressed by Celia's accomplishments with the ACS, offered her a seat on its Governing Council. In 1976 she was made the organization's president, and a year later she served as its executive director, becoming the first woman to head a national environmental organization. During that same period, in 1972, she was also appointed to the Federal-State Land Use Commission for Alaska.

In the meantime, Celia and Ginny continued to operate Camp Denali and lead wilderness treks and other programs. Finally in 1975, being up to their eyeballs in political activities, the pair decided to sell the camp. They did not want to turn it over to just anyone, however. A developer, they feared, would likely tear the camp down to build a hotel on the site. Instead, they transferred ownership to neighbors Wally and Jerryne Cole, with no down payment. The women knew that the Coles would continue to manage Camp Denali in the same tradition. Members of the Cole family have operated the camp ever since.

In 1980 Congress passed the Alaska National Interest Lands Conservation Act, which Celia, Ginny, and others had spent more than a decade fighting for. The law, which created ten new national parks in the state and enlarged three others, protected 56 million acres of Arctic wilderness. It was called "the most significant land conservation measure in the history of our nation."

Shortly after the ANILCA passed, Celia and Ginny decided to dissolve the Alaska Conservation Society. At the same time, Celia created the Alaska Conservation Foundation, through which the pair divided the society's remaining funds among several other Alaska conservation groups. This was hardly the end of Celia and Ginny's activism, however. Both women continued writing conservation articles and letters to officials in support of environmental projects and legislation. Since 1979, Celia had been writing a column for the *Fairbanks Daily News-Miner.* Her "fearless and outspoken" editorials brought a more progressive viewpoint to the otherwise conservative, pro-development newspaper. Ginny, too, wrote a regular column, beginning in 1982. Called "From the Woodpile," it appeared in the newletter of the Northern Alaska Environmental Center, an organization Ginny had helped found in 1971. Both women's columns ran for more than twenty years.

Beginning in the mid-1980s, Celia and Ginny, together and separately, were showered with awards and honors in recognition of their decades of dedication to Alaska conservation. In 1985 the Alaska Conservation Foundation created the Celia Hunter Award for Outstanding Volunteer Contributions. The first recipient? Ginny Hill Wood. The ACF also established the Celia M. Hunter Fund, which provided grants for students majoring in environmental subjects. In 1991 the Sierra Club bestowed its highest honor, the John Muir Award, jointly to Celia and Ginny. Seven years later, Celia received the prestigious Robert Marshall Award from the Wilderness Society.

Still active in their eighties, Celia (left) and Ginny take a hike near their home in Dogpatch. This picture was taken in 2001, a few months before Celia's death. —Courtesy Jenna Hertz, Flickr Creative Commons

And in 2001, the two women shared the Alaska Conservation Foundation's first Lifetime Achievement Award. This would be the last honor Celia would accept in person.

Active to the end, Celia continued her work to preserve Alaska's wilderness almost to the moment of her death. On the evening of December 1, 2001, at her log cabin in Dogpatch, Celia was busy writing letters to senators in Washington, urging them to oppose oil drilling in the Arctic National Wildlife Refuge, the park she and Ginny had helped become a reality. Then she went to bed and, sometime during the night, Celia Hunter died in her sleep. She was eighty-two.

Needless to say, Ginny was crushed at the loss of her dearest friend. "I am missing you in ways and places I could not have imagined," she wrote. "I miss your laughter bursts; your insufferable cheerfulness so early on dark, bleak days; your willingness to tackle any problem—mechanical, societal, or environmental—undaunted."

Upon hearing of her death, Washington state Representative Jay Inslee paid tribute to Celia in a speech before Congress. Inslee noted that "Our national parks, our wildlife refuges, and our national forests in Alaska have come to be heirlooms that we may pass on to our children and their children in large part because of Celia Hunter."

Six months after Celia's death, Ginny took some of her best friend's ashes to Camp Denali's fiftieth anniversary celebration and spread them on the ridge that overlooked the camp and the mountain. Another friend took the rest of the ashes and placed pinches of them in various wilderness locations in the Lower Forty-eight. In 2009 Celia Hunter was posthumously inducted into the Alaska Women's Hall of Fame; Ginny Wood was inducted two years later.

Ginny carried on, staying active both physically and politically. She led wilderness treks into her seventies, skiied into her eighties, and gardened into her nineties. In 2009 Ginny won the Florence Collins Award from the Northern Alaska Environmental Center, and the next year she received the U.S. Fish and Wildlife Service's Citizen Award for Exceptional Service. Also in 2010, Congress honored Ginny and her fellow surviving WASPs with a Congressional Gold Medal. A biography of Ginny called *Boots, Bikes, and Bombers*, based on Karen Brewster's extended interviews with her, was published in 2012. Finally, on March 8, 2013, Ginny Wood died peacefully, surrounded by friends, in her Dogpatch cabin. She was ninety-five.

These two intrepid visionaries, Celia Hunter and Ginny Hill Wood, had an astounding impact not only on the Fairbanks area and the state of Alaska, but on the entire nation and, indeed, the whole planet. Yet the greatest part of their legacy may be the way they have inspired others to keep fighting to preserve wild places in Alaska and throughout the globe.

NORA GUINN

"Fairness and Justice for All"

In southwestern Alaska, where the Yukon and Kuskokwim Rivers twist their way to the Bering Sea, lies the vast Yukon-Kuskokwim Delta, composed of treeless tundra, lakes, and wetlands. To this day the delta remains virtually roadless, and many of its Native Alaskan residents still live simple, traditional lives of fishing, hunting, and gathering edible wild plants. It was in this region that Nora Venes (later Nora Guinn) was born, grew up, raised her nine children, and became Alaska's first Native American district court judge.

Nora was born in the tiny village of Akiak, on the Kuskokwim River, on November 11, 1920, to Joe and Anna (or Annie) Venes. She was the first of the couple's three children. Joe was a Norwegian immigrant who had been among the thousands of Klondike gold seekers who came to Canada's Yukon Territory in 1897. He later settled in the village of Akiak, where he ran a bunkhouse for area miners. Here he met Anna, a local Yu'pik Eskimo about twenty-five years his junior. The couple married, probably in the late 1910s, and remained in Akiak. By 1930, Joe owned a carpentry shop in the village. Most people in Akiak spoke Yu'pik, so Nora and her brothers grew up bilingual.

Nora and her two younger brothers, Joe Jr. and Elias, attended school in Akiak through the eighth grade, but there was no high school in the village, nor was there one in Bethel, the delta's commercial hub, about forty miles east. Eskimo students wanting a secondary education had to attend one of three industrial boarding schools established for Native Alaskans by the territorial government. The schools were designed, according to then-governor George Parks, to offer "training, encouragement, and hope to exceptional young people." Of the three schools, the closest one to Akiak was about four hundred miles east, in the Athabaskan village of Eklutna, just north of the new railroad town of Anchorage.

Nora Venes, age fifteen, in Eklutna
—Courtesy Susan Guinn Murphy

When Nora arrived at Eklutna in the early 1930s, it was the first time she had been away from home. She was one of some ninety teenagers housed in the school's three-story dormitories. In addition to academic classes, students were taught farming as well as traditional Native skills. Girls learned to weave baskets and sew beaded moccasins, while boys learned to tan reindeer hides, set traplines, and mend fishing nets. Extracurricular activities included the 4-H club, which taught students not only farming skills but also parliamentary procedure. The school offered opportunities for fun, too. Students ice-skated on a nearby lake in the winter, and in the summer they hiked and picnicked.

During the three years Nora was at the Eklutna school, one of her closest friends was Sadie Brower, an Inupiaq Eskimo from Barrow, the northernmost village in Alaska. When the girls left Eklutna to finish high school in the States—Sadie in southern California, Nora in Portland, Oregon—they would have been amazed to know what the future held for them. Some twenty-five years later, Sadie Brower Neakok and Nora Venes Guinn became two of the first women and first Native Alaskans to serve as magistrates in Alaska's justice system.

Nora attended her senior year of high school in Portland. A much-respected physician in Akiak, Dr. George, was leaving Alaska after many years and returning to practice in Oregon. He invited Nora to stay with his family there, helping them as a babysitter for their children, while she finished school.

Meanwhile, while Nora was in Portland, a red-haired Irishman named Charlie Guinn arrived in Bethel in 1938. Born in South Dakota in 1917, Charlie grew up in Yakima, Washington. At age twenty-one, seeking adventure, he headed for Alaska and ended up in the Yukon-Kuskokwim Delta. He was living in Bethel when Nora returned home from Portland in the summer of 1940. Shortly afterward, Charlie introduced himself to Nora, and they were married seven months later, in January 1941.

The newlyweds lived in Bethel and Akiak until August 1942, when Charlie took a job as a teacher for the Bureau of Indian Affairs (BIA) in Tununak, 115 miles to the west on Alaska's southwestern coast. By then Nora had given birth to the couple's first child, Susan, born in September of 1941. Tununak, the westernmost of three fishing villages on Nelson Island, faced the Bering Sea. When the Guinns arrived there, the United States had just entered World War II, and the Japanese invasion of the nearby Aleutian Islands on June 3, 1942, had shown the territory's western coast to be vulnerable to attack. In response, the U.S. military organized a reserve force of unpaid volunteers, the Alaska Territorial Guard, to guard the coastline. In Tununak, Charlie signed up.

For the Guinns and the other residents of Nelson Island, blackouts and fighter planes flying overhead became the norm. At the BIA school, Nora and Charlie found they were needed not only to teach, but to provide health services in their tiny community, where the war made professional assistance even more difficult to get than before. In fact, Charlie himself, assisting a Yu'pik midwife named Rosalie Hooper, helped deliver the Guinns' next two children, Charles Jr. (born 1943) and John (born 1944), in Tununak.

At the war's end in 1945, the Guinns returned to Bethel, where the family spent the next five years. Charlie worked for an assortment of employers in Bethel, including Alaska Star Airlines. During that time another son, Robert, was born in 1947. Sadly, only twenty-three years later, Robert was killed in a car accident.

In 1950 the Guinns moved 120 miles north to Marshall, on the Yukon River, to operate a general store. Eldest daughter Susan Guinn (now Susan Murphy) remembered the two and a half years in Marshall as the most enjoyable place they lived. There were no roads, no cars or vehicles. "We walked everywhere," Susan said. In summer the children picked berries—blueberries, raspberries, crowberries. Marshall is still sometimes called "Alaska's best-kept secret" for the quality of its berries. Nora kept busy not only helping to run the store and looking after her children, but also tending to the health needs of the community, nursing the sick, delivering babies, or whatever was needed.

In 1952 the Guinn family returned to Bethel to stay. Not long after the move, the Guinns welcomed another child, Judy, born in 1952.

In Bethel, Charlie again worked for the Bureau of Indian Affairs school system, managing the maintenance of BIA schools and properties throughout the area, a job that required much traveling. Meanwhile Nora, who had developed an interest in village government, learned of a job opening with the territorial court for a United States Commissioner to serve the Bethel area.

Before Alaska was made a state, the federal government set up a commissioner system to serve the judicial needs of the territory's far-flung population. A commissioner's duties were similar to those of a justice of the peace: issuing licenses; keeping records; handling hearings, misdemeanor criminal cases, and small claims; and performing civil duties such as officiating marriages. Commissioners, who didn't need to be lawyers or even have a law background, were chosen and appointed by a district court judge. Nora applied for the position in the mid-1950s and was appointed.

As Nora's professional and civic responsibilities grew, so did the size of her family. Margaret was born in 1955, James in 1960, Shelley in 1962, and the youngest, Cindy, arrived in 1963. "My mother was pretty capable," Susan said, "both as a parent and as a commissioner. And we all helped." Because of the twenty-two-year span between the firstborn, Susan, and her youngest sibling, Cindy, there were always older children to look after younger ones. In addition, the Guinns' home was always open to local kids who needed help.

After Alaska became a state in 1959, the federal court's commissioner system was replaced by a state court that used a magistrate system. Local magistrates, who were appointed by an Alaska Superior Court judge, provided essentially the same services as commissioners had, but their responsiblities were outlined more formally. Like commissioners, magistrates did not have to be lawyers and needed only a high school education, but upon their appointment, they were trained by the state in a two-week-long seminar.

No doubt due to her commissioner experience, Nora was appointed Bethel's first magistrate, the only judicial officer in the growing town and its surrounding district. As a commissioner and as a magistrate, she mostly learned on the job, but she also read great amounts of legal reference materials. By all accounts, Nora used common sense and creativity in her courtroom and was sensitive to the Native citizens' cultural values. Many who came before her bench spoke very little English, so Nora, fluent in Yu'pik as well as English, held proceedings in both languages as needed.

In addition to the language barrier, Native defendants often had ideas of guilt and punishment that differed from those of the American legal system. Nora tried to explain to them the charges against them and the process of trials, rulings, and sentencing. Sitting in her courtroom has been described as "an educational experience."

One of Nora's colleagues, the late Christopher Cooke, who was a lawyer at the time but later became a superior court judge, remembered that Nora demanded respect in her courtroom. When as a young attorney he first appeared before her without a necktie, she insisted that lawyers coming into her court should look like lawyers. "I cleaned up my act," Cooke said. Cooke also praised Nora for educating attorneys and law enforcement officers "about the Native way of doing and looking at things, and about fairness and justice for all."

Nora served Bethel as a magistrate until 1967. Later that year, she was appointed to a new post with even broader responsibilities—district court judge for the Bethel District Court. She was the first Native Alaskan and one of the first women to be given a district judgeship; she was also one of the few non-lawyers ever appointed to that office. In this position, Nora not only continued her courtroom teachings, she also worked to help non–Native Alaskan officials realize the difficulty that Yu'pik speakers had understanding what was happening in the courtroom. At Alaska's first judicial conference in 1970, Judge Guinn, giving the opening address, spoke for five minutes as the attendees looked increasingly confused—she had delivered her introduction entirely in Yu'pik. When she finished, she asked the audience members how they felt, pointing out that their bewilderment was exactly what Eskimo people feel in English-speaking courtrooms.

Judge Nora Guinn in her office, 1967 —Courtesy Susan Guinn Murphy

At one of the conferences she attended, Nora was surprised—and delighted—to meet her old friend from her Eklutna school days, Sadie Brower, now Sadie Neakok and a fellow magistrate. As the magistrate for Barrow, Sadie shared Nora's concerns about the Native people they served—Sadie the Inupiaq Eskimos, Nora the Yu'pik. Both faced a shortage of police and support services in their communities, and alcoholism among Native Alaskans was a major problem in both Bethel and Barrow, as it was throughout the state. Nora's family remembered Sadie as a close family friend. The two often called each other to discuss common issues, especially the alcohol crisis that was ravaging Eskimo communities.

Bethel had passed a local law prohibiting liquor, but it could not be enforced due to its conflict with state law. By 1970 Nora estimated that 95 percent of the cases she heard were alcohol related. The Bethel district was also said to have one of the nation's highest per capita rates of suicide, homicide, and domestic violence, as well as the lowest per capita income. Furthermore, the district had only two state police officers, who were responsible for serving the entire 93,000-square-mile region. It was obvious to many Bethel citizens that something needed to be done. With Nora's help, the village council proposed establishing a "sleep-off center" where intoxicated citizens could be taken to sober up instead of being jailed. "It was our first attempt to face the drinking problem head on," Nora said. "We didn't have funding, so we made do with what we had."

Volunteers formed a nonprofit group, Bethel Community Services, an organization unique in the state. Trooper John Malone agreed to oversee the Sleep-off Center program. The National Guard donated fifty sleeping bags for the center, which opened in a remodeled trailer in June 1971. It was called *Ekaiyurvik*, which means "place of help" in Yu'pik. Funding came from various welfare and health agencies as well as the city of Bethel; eventually the state and federal governments kicked in funds too. Rehabilitation, rather than jail, was the center's goal, and a staff composed of recovered alcoholics, all of them Eskimo, was hired to provide counseling and education. The center's early case load was described as "staggering." Yet the center reported significant successes, such as a drop in alcohol-related deaths from fourteen in 1971 to four the following year.

Today, the services provided by Bethel Community Services—including the alcoholism program, renamed the Sobering Center—are administered by the Yukon-Kuskokwim Health Corporation. The funding arm of the organization, Bethel Community Services Foundation, still exists, and over the years it has supported local programs to help children, people with mental-health problems, the elderly, and people with disabilities.

In 1971 Nora was appointed Special Master of the Family Division of the Alaska Supreme Court, in which post she heard cases

The Guinn family, 1979. Back row, left to right: Susan, Shelley, Charlie, Nora, Judy, Margie, and Cindy; front: Charles Jr., John, and Jimmy —Courtesy Susan Guinn Murphy

that involved the placement of at-risk children, an assignment dear to her heart. Often, she would take a troubled child into her own home. During this period, Nora also taught training sessions for other judges and magistrates.

Nora retired from the bench in 1976, but she remained active in community organizations, particularly those involving children's welfare. In 1978 she received an honorary Doctor of Law degree from the University of Alaska, Anchorage. Numerous other honors and awards followed, including the First Lady Volunteer Award in 1979, the Alaska Native Woman of the Year in 1983, and Callista's Citizen of the Year in 1984. In 1994, concerned that elderly Eskimos had to go to an Anchorage facility—four hundred miles away—when they became old or sick, Nora began raising funds to build a nursing home in Bethel, beginning with $50,000 out of her own pocket. After a decade of planning, the Yukon-Kuskokwim Elder's Home opened in 2013, eight years after Nora's death.

In the last years of her life, an eye disease called macular degeneration limited what Nora was able to do. Before Charlie's death on December 31, 1993, the Guinns spent winters in Mexico, but Alaska was still home. Several of the Guinn children remained in the Bethel area to raise their own families, so Nora was often occupied with her grandchildren—of which she had thirty-one by the time she died—and her great-grandchildren, who by 2005 numbered thirty-three.

After she died on July 6, 2005, at age eighty-four, Judge Nora Guinn was memorialized by many people in many ways. In 2007 the Alaska Bar Association established the Judge Nora Guinn Award, presented annually to an Alaskan "who has made an extraordinary or sustained effort to assist Alaska's Bush residents, especially its Native population, overcome language and cultural barriers to obtaining justice through the legal system." In Bethel, the city council unanimously voted to name their new courthouse building after

Nora in her later years —Courtesy Susan Guinn Murphy

Nora. The formal unveiling took place on August 25, 2009. At the dedication, Bethel's mayor praised Nora for working diligently "to improve communication and understanding" between the legal system and Alaska Natives. Also in 2009, Nora was inducted into the Alaska Women's Hall of Fame for achievement in law.

One of the best descriptions of Nora Guinn's character came from Judge Christopher Cooke, who succeeded her in the Bethel District Court following her retirement. In her obituary for the Alaska Bar Association, he wrote:

> Although fluent in two languages, there was one word Judge Guinn apparently did not know: the word CAN'T. Undoubtedly along the way there were those who said, "You can't be a judge because you're a woman," or "You can't because you are a Native," or "You can't because you don't have a college degree or a law school education." But these obstacles didn't stop Nora Guinn. Hidden within her tiny frame was fierce determination and an iron will which enabled her to do whatever she set her mind to, and showing that she didn't believe in the word CAN'T. She could, and she did.

THELMA BUCHHOLDT
A Filipina in Alaska

Thelma Garcia was born 5,000 miles from Alaska. Growing up, she never dreamed of going there. She probably did not expect ever to leave her homeland, the Philippines, much less to settle in the Last Frontier. Yet circumstances and twists of fate not only landed Thelma in Alaska but kept her there—the forty-ninth state became her unlikely home and the wellspring of her career as a politician and her life's work as a civil-rights activist.

Thelma Juana Garcia was born on August 1, 1934, in Claveria, the northernmost town on the Philippine mainland, in the province of Cagayan. The black-sand beaches of this fishing village, bordering the China Sea, were noted for their beauty, and Filipinos often referred to Claveria as the "Coastal Paradise of the Cagayan North."

Thelma's parents represented two different Filipino tribal heritages. Her father, Eugenio Manalo Garcia, was half Ibanag (or Ybanag) and half Aeta (or Agta). The Ibanag, the original inhabitants of the Cagayan Valley, were an agricultural people who dwelled along the Cagayan River. The Aetas were nomadic mountain people. Thelma's mother, Dionisia de Leon, was of Ilocano (or Ilokano) descent. Originally from the western coast of Luzon, the main island, the Ilocano migrated northeast to the Cagayan Valley in the mid-1800s and soon became the dominant culture. With their strong European Catholic roots, the Ilocanos tended to look down on the darker complexioned, less affluent minorities—especially the mountain tribes such as the Aeta and the Igorots—whom they considered to be of a lower class.

Thelma's mother Dionisia (Diony) was born in Claveria, the youngest child in a wealthy family. Thelma's father was Eugenio Garcia, a skilled sailor from a poor family in nearby Pamplona. Eugenio worked for Diony's grandmother, piloting the De Leons' trading boat. When he began to court Diony, her family would have objected to the match except for one thing—Dionisia was already thirty years old, a pitiable old maid. Even a dark-skinned, under-class husband was better than none. The pair married on May 8, 1933, and settled in Claveria.

Eugenio did not make much money, but Diony contributed to the Garcia family's income with several businesses her own family had set her up with. Thelma, born in 1934, was the first of the couple's six children (four girls and two boys). Some of Thelma's earliest memories were happy ones of sailing aboard the family boat with her parents. Growing up, Thelma learned Tagalog (the main language of the Philippines), Ilocano (the language of her mother's people), and English.

The Garcias' life changed abruptly with the advent of World War II. Just days after Japanese flyers attacked Pearl Harbor, Hawaii, in December 1941, Japan invaded the Philippines, with detachments moving into Claveria. Enemy officers took over the Garcia family's home, near the center of the village, to serve as their headquarters. Thelma was seven years old. The family escaped upriver into the surrounding hill country to wait out the end of the war, which would finally come three and a half years later.

Before the invasion, Thelma had begun classes at the Academy of St. Joseph in Clevaria, but the rural mountain community they fled to had no schools, so her formal education was postponed until the war's end. When the Garcias returned to Claveria in 1945, Thelma, age ten, reenrolled at St. Joseph. Fortunately, she was exceedingly bright and a quick learner, and she made up for the lost years. By the time she was sixteen, she had completed high school at St. Joseph, where she was the official class historian, and was looking forward to college. But where would she go, and how?

Diony's brother, Fermin de Leon, a well-to-do chef in Las Vegas, Nevada, arranged to sponsor Thelma's education in the States. In the fall of 1951, she would be enrolling at Mount St. Mary's College in Brentwood, California, a Los Angeles suburb. As Thelma gazed out the window of the plane from Manila to L.A.—the seventeen-year-old's first flight—her aerial view of the Philippines' capital was the last she would see of her homeland for many years. When Thelma arrived in Los Angeles, her Uncle Fermin took her to the campus in Brentwood, and her new life began.

Shortly after graduating from Mount St. Mary's in the spring of 1956, with a degree in zoology, Thelma went to stay with her uncle in Las Vegas, expecting to return to the Philippines later that year. In the meantime, she decided to take some classes at what was then called Nevada Southern University (now the University of Nevada, Las Vegas). Since her studies at Mount St. Mary's had been science oriented, Thelma thought that some liberal-arts courses would fill gaps in her education. It would also keep her student visa active until she could return at the end of the semester to Claveria, where her parents planned for her to take over a family business. That fall, she signed up for night classes in English Literature and beginning French.

When Thelma walked into her French class, at least one fellow student, Jon Buchholdt, took notice. Jon, originally from Salt

Lake City, Utah, had joined the Navy a year earlier and had been assigned to the new Lake Mead Naval Base near Las Vegas. On duty during the day, he took classes in the evening. Upon seeing this pretty and slender young woman, who was so petite that her Mount St. Mary's classmates had called her "Thumbelina," Jon was not shy about asking her out.

Together Jon and Thelma explored the newly built hotels on the Las Vegas Strip. They didn't gamble, but they enjoyed the free food that the hotels offered to promote their restaurants and the evening shows they could watch for the price of one drink each. One time, they sat in the audience of the first-ever Jerry Lewis fundraiser for muscular dystrophy.

By Christmas, Jon and Thelma were engaged, and Thelma gave up her plan to return to the Philippines. In planning the wedding, they discovered a major stumbling block. Jon was white, and it was illegal in Nevada—as it was in most other states in those days—for couples of different races to marry. The only exception was California. Thelma hoped that the chaplain at Mount St. Mary's, her old school in Brentwood, would marry them, but, legal or not, the priest refused to perform an interracial ceremony. Finally the pair went to Santa Monica, where they were married in a civil courthouse ceremony on June 14, 1957. Thelma's parents were upset when they learned that their daughter's marriage had not been sanctified by the Catholic Church. To make amends, Thelma and Jon exchanged vows a year later in a church ceremony conducted by a Filipino priest in Los Angeles.

When Jon's stint with the Navy ended, shortly after their courthouse wedding, the newlyweds moved to the Los Angeles area. Thelma took a job teaching at St. Marks School, a Catholic elementary school, while Jon enrolled for classes at Loyola-Marymount University. Jon had found an apartment close to campus, but when the landlord discovered that Thelma was a Filipina, he suddenly "remembered" that he'd already rented the unit to someone else. It was a prime example of the rampant racial discrimination that would launch the civil-rights movement of the 1960s.

Jon and Thelma's first child, daughter Titania, was born in Los Angeles on March 13, 1958. Sons Chris and Hans followed, in 1959 and 1962 respectively. In 1963, fed up with racial discrimination, Thelma and Jon helped organize a group called Catholics United for Racial Equality (CURE), the first civil-rights organization in the Los Angeles area. It was Thelma's first experience with political activism, and she learned some of the community-organizing and media skills that would later serve her well as a politician.

After Jon's graduation from Loyola-Marymount in 1964, he was offered a job as a field epidemiologist by the Communicable Disease Center (later renamed the Center for Disease Control, now called Centers for Disease Control and Prevention). He was assigned to Schenectady, New York, so the Buchholdts moved there for what would be a yearlong stay. Then in 1965, Jon volunteered to lead a measles-eradication program in rural Alaska, and off the family went to the Northland. Little did they suspect that the recently admitted state would become their permanent home.

The Buchholdts settled in Anchorage, though Jon traveled extensively to rural villages with the measles program. During their first year in Alaska, the family welcomed a fourth child, a boy named Dylan. Thelma, busy looking after her family, still found time for community involvement. As a parent and former teacher, she was concerned by the lack of supervised after-school activities for children in fast-growing Anchorage. In 1966 she helped establish a local chapter of the Boys Club of America (later renamed the Boys and Girls Clubs of America), which offered sports and arts programs. Thelma also did volunteer work with the March of Dimes and the League of Women Voters.

Also in the 1960s, Thelma joined the Filipino Community of Anchorage, Alaska, Inc. (FCAA), a group whose stated purpose is, among other things, to "promote and perpetuate Filipino cultural heritage" in the Anchorage area. Thelma had not had much contact with other Filipinos until one afternoon, while shopping in downtown Anchorage, she saw a notice in a store window for a Filipino dinner sponsored by the Filipino Community of Anchorage. The group, which began meeting at informal picnics and potlucks in the late 1950s, had formally organized in 1965. Thelma quickly became involved in its activities.

During the same period, in the late 1960s, Thelma became politically active on a broader scale, joining the Anchorage Ad Hoc Committee of Young Democrats, which was formed to reinvigorate the party. In 1969 she was among the Young Democrats chosen to attend a series of seminars entitled "The Future Of Alaska," sponsored by the Brookings Institution. The conference, which met in Anchorage, covered many topics, including economic development, education, and conservation in the state.

Meanwhile in 1969, Jon left the Communicable Disease Center to become manager of the Anchorage branch of the recently created, federally funded Community Action Agency (CAA). This nonprofit organization was formed in 1966 to direct programs to help poor rural residents throughout the nation. In his position as manager of the Greater Anchorage Area CAA, Jon hoped to address some of the problems he'd observed in his health-care work with rural Native Alaskans. His first proposal was to establish health services for senior citizens living in outlying villages. Upon winning the funding for his program, Jon enlisted the help of Eben Hopson, the executive director of the Alaska Federation of Natives (AFN), to establish clinics in Native villages. Hopson, a former state senator from Barrow, was a highly respected Native leader. Together

*Thelma in
Native costume,
date unknown*
—Courtesy Jon
Buchholdt

Jon, Eben, and others established the first clinic in Bethel; later they built another one in Nome. Hopson remained a close family friend of Jon and Thelma until his death in 1979.

Thelma's involvement with the Filipino Community of Anchorage continued, and in 1971 she became the organization's first female president, a position she held for two terms. As president, Thelma was responsible for arranging the group's annual banquet, which included Filipino entertainment. Traditional Filipino folk dances had always been featured at the event, but the program never included the tribal dances of the Igorots, a minority group who were discriminated against in the Philippines just as her father's people, the Aetas, were. While she was organizing a group of Igorot dancers to perform at the banquet, Thelma developed an abiding interest in the dances of the mountain peoples, and she later helped establish a permanent Igorot dance troupe in Anchorage. In the mid-1970s, to further promote pride in all the various indigenous ethnic groups of the Philippines, Thelma founded the Filipino Heritage Council of Alaska.

During the election year of 1972, Thelma's skills in community organizing led to several politically important appointments. For one, she was named vice chairwoman of the Alaska delegation to the 1972 Democratic Convention. Also that year, the Democratic presidential nominee, Senator George McGovern, chose Thelma to be the Alaska coordinator for his campaign. Although McGovern lost his presidential bid to Republican Richard Nixon in November, Thelma gained invaluable political experience and statewide recognition during the campaign. In addition, due to her demonstrated commitment to the welfare of Native Alaskans, Thelma was appointed to the Alaska State Advisory Committee to the U.S. Commission on Civil Rights in 1972. She was vocal in her support of Alaskan Native land claims, even though this position was not politically popular with mainstream America at the time. Thelma would serve on the advisory committee for more than three decades.

In 1974 Thelma, now with significant political experience under her belt, decided to run for a seat in Alaska's House of Representatives. Although most of the voters in her district were white—only 3 percent were Asian American—she won the election. With this victory, Thelma Buchholdt became the first Asian American of either sex ever elected to the Alaska legislature, and the first-ever Filipina American legislator in the United States. She was reelected three times, in 1976, 1978, and 1980. During her tenure, she was a member of the House Finance Committee, later serving as its first female vice chairman. As a committee member, Thelma advocated funding for recreational and cultural centers; for small business loans and student loans; programs for seniors, health, and education; and

Alaska State Representative Thelma Buchholdt, 1979
—Alaska State Library, Portrait File, ASL-P01-1255

for building and improving roads, trails, and local parks. After 1980, oil production brought huge revenues to the state, and Thelma worked to made sure that the monies were distributed fairly. Later, in 1987, Thelma would become the first Asian American to be elected president of the National Order of Women Legislators.

Even while busy campaigning for her first term in the Alaska House, Thelma continued pursuing causes of personal importance. In 1976 she and Jon helped organize the Alaska Eskimo Whaling Commission (AEWC). The following year, at the International Whaling Convention in Tokyo, Thelma explained the commission's objections to outlawing the traditional Eskimo subsistence hunting of bowhead whales. As a state legislator, Thelma was able to help the commission's efforts by winning funding for an underwater bio-acoustical study of Alaska's bowhead whale population. From this and other studies, the AEWC was able to create a management plan to preserve the animals and their habitat.

The year 1980 was also a busy one for Thelma. In addition to running her reelection campaign, she helped coordinate the first statewide Filipino Community Leadership Conference, held in Juneau in April. In August she addressed the first national Asian-Pacific Women's Conference in Washington, D.C. Also in 1980, Thelma began fundraising efforts for the Asian Alaskan Cultural Center, which was officially organized as a nonprofit group in 1983 "to promote mutal respect and understanding of Asian and American cultures." Based in Anchorage, the center raised money for high school scholarships, cultural events, and bilingual education programs for Asian Americans in Alaska. The center's headquarters, built inside a local elementary school, opened in 1988.

After losing her bid for reelection to the Alaska House in 1982, Thelma left politics, but she became director of the state legislature's Anchorage office. She also continued with her nonprofit work. By 1988 her children were all grown, and both Thelma and Jon began to consider a career change. Their eldest, daughter Titania, had applied for law school that year at Georgetown University Law Center in Washington, D.C. Both Thelma and Jon decided to join her, enrolling at the District of Columbia School of Law. All three Buchholdts graduated in 1991 and, upon returning to Alaska, were admitted to the Alaska Bar Association. Thelma and Jon established a private practice in Anchorage, the Buchholdt Law Offices, specializing in family law. Titania later moved to California and set up her own practice there. Thelma and Jon's youngest son, Dylan, later became a lawyer as well, practicing in Anchorage. Christopher and Hans also remained in Alaska; Chris went into finance and Hans became a geographer.

In 1994 Governor Tony Knowles appointed Thelma executive director of the Alaska Office of Equal Employment Opportunity; she would serve in that position until 2002. Meanwhile, her interest in Filipino culture and history continued to grow, and in 1994 she founded the Alaska chapter of the Filipino American National Historical Society (FANHS). Her involvement in this and other Filipino organizations fed her fascination with, and curiosity about, the part Filipinos played in Alaska's history. Finding little had been written on this topic, Thelma set out to write a book of her own.

In researching the book, Thelma traveled extensively, consulting thousands of records in archives throughout the United States and interviewing older Filipinos and their children for personal stories. The result was *Filipinos in Alaska: 1788–1958*, a two-hundred-page volume published by the Asian Alaskan Cultural Center in 1996. The book's purpose, Thelma wrote, was "to lay the foundation for a continuing effort to research and document Filipino history in Alaska, to teach Alaska's children about the Filipino discovery and development of Alaska, and to strengthen Filipino identity and sense of place and public esteem." She also produced a thirty-minute documentary film on the subject. The year her book came out, Thelma's alma mater, Mount St. Mary's College in California, presented her with an Outstanding Alumna Award for Community Service.

By 2000, Thelma, still serving as director of the Office of Equal Employment Opportunity as well as practicing law privately, was tapped by Governor Tony Knowles to also direct the governor's

Thelma Buchholdt, Executive Director, Alaska Equal Employment Office, 2002 —Courtesy Jon Buchholdt

office in Anchorage. In 2001 the governor again called upon Thelma, this time to serve, with thirteen other ethnic-minority leaders, on his Governor's Commission on Tolerance "to explore racism in the state."

In 2004, along with her daughter Titania and son Chris, Thelma returned to the Philippines to visit Thelma's family and see again the beautiful countryside of her girlhood. In addition to Thelma's hometown of Claveria, the Buchholdts visited the mountain town of Guinaang, where the villagers had prepared a ceremonial welcome and a celebration at which local singers and dancers performed.

Afterward, Thelma arranged for a number of mountain tribal dancers to perform in Claveria while she was there. Titania became
deeply involved with indigenous Filipino music and dance, performing and teaching workshops in California and throughout the
United States and the Philippines. Two years later, Thelma again
returned to the Philippines, this time with Jon, and had another
wonderful visit with friends and family.

The following year, 2007, Thelma was making plans for the
upcoming national conference of the Filipino American National
Historical Society, scheduled for July 2008 in Anchorage. She saw
the event as an opportunity for Filipinos from different states to
share knowledge and culture. In September 2007, Thelma wrote
to the society's members with an update on the conference. All
arrangements were in place, she said, and she was confident that
the event would be a success. But she closed her letter with heart-
breaking news—she had just been diagnosed with terminal cancer
of the pancreas. She hoped, however, that she would still be able to
take part in the conference. Sadly, that did not happen.

Thelma Garcia Buchholdt died at home on November 5, 2007.
She was seventy-three. In accordance with her request, Thelma's
family buried her in the tribal costume of her native land. Services
were held in Anchorage and in the Philippines.

The day after Thelma died, then-governor Sarah Palin declared
that November 10, 2007, would be celebrated as Thelma Buchholdt Day in Alaska. Later, the city of Anchorage proclaimed a local
Thelma Buchholdt Day, which would take place on July 5, 2008,
in acknowledgement of Thelma's "lifetime commitment to public
services that upholds social justice and the great values of cultural
diversity and respect for all peoples."

A year after her death, the Alaska Democratic Party posthumously
honored Thelma with the James Doogan Lifetime Achievement
Award. In 2009 she was inducted into the Alaska Women's Hall of

Fame. The following year, the Filipino community in Anchorage built a pavilion in Woodland Park to honor her. The Thelma G. Buchholdt Picnic Shelter was dedicated on June 12, 2010.

MARY
SHIELDS
Trails and Tails

On any given summer morning, in the Goldstream Valley about twelve miles north of Fairbanks, Mary Shields might be spied picking raspberries from the vines she planted on the sod roof of her log cabin. Or one might find her in her yard, laughing as her five dogs leap around her feet, barking happily.

As of 2014, Mary has lived in this beautiful, hand-built, one-room home with its large windows and surrounding gardens for more than twenty-five years. Retired since 1991 from her career as a long-distance musher and racer, Mary now welcomes small tour groups to see her little slice of paradise and observe firsthand the tender care she gives her sled dogs, who seem to enjoy the guests as much as she does. The five canines—Too Sweet, O.J., Crockett, Frosty-Frosty, and Big Boy—are the most recent in a succession of dogs that Mary has raised and loved over the years.

Mary Shields was born on October 12, 1944, in Waukesha, Wisconsin. Her mother, Leah, was a physical-education teacher, and her father, Clyde, was a high school principal. She had one brother, Tom, who was a year older. Growing up, Mary loved hiking, bicycling, baseball, and most of all, swimming. Although she never had a childhood pet of her own, Mary loved animals. Some of her fondest memories were of visits to her grandmother's dairy farm in central Wisconsin, with its milk cows, chickens, and work horses. When she was old enough, Mary was allowed to lead the horses to the water trough at the end of each day.

In the summers during high school, Mary worked as a lifeguard at the school's pool. After graduating in 1962, she enrolled at the University of Wisconsin in Madison, signing up for whatever classes interested her. She realized years later that taking classes in so many different disciplines had helped prepare her for her future of self-employment.

At the end of her junior year at the university, looking for a summer job, Mary saw a help-wanted ad for counselors in a Campfire Girls day-camp program to teach swimming and other skills to girls in rural Alaska. She'd never been a Campfire Girl, but she had been a Girl Scout and had participated in similar outdoor-oriented programs. The opportunity sounded like an adventure, and Mary liked adventure. She applied and got the job, which included transportation to and from Alaska.

Arriving in Fairbanks in June 1965, Mary fell hopelessly in love with Alaska at first sight. The Campfire Girls' traveling program took her from village to village in the western part of the state, where she was captivated by the wilderness and the simple Alaskan way of life. When summer ended, she could hardly wait to return. After earning her science degree in June 1966, Mary eagerly accepted a new Campfire Girls assignment in the North. "Three days after my last exam, I departed for Alaska," she recalled, not even staying for the commencement ceremony.

Mary's job this time was to direct sailing and swimming programs at the Campfire Girls' camp on Kenai Lake, in south-central Alaska. Upon arriving, she noticed one immediate problem: the camp had no sailboats. She told her employers that she knew a boat builder in Madison who could sell her some small, one-sail dinghies. The Campfire Girls gave her money to buy three boats, but the organization did not have the funds to have them shipped to Alaska. Calling a sailboat racer she knew in California, Mary described the problem, and the man volunteered to pay to air-mail the three dinghies to Alaska.

By summer's end, Mary was convinced that her future lay in Alaska. Although she had no job and no place to live, she was determined to stay in Fairbanks. By winter she had found a position with a local family, the Lawlors, who let her live in an outbuilding in exchange for babysitting the youngest of their nine children. For spending money, Mary did various odd jobs around town. In her spare time, she hiked through nearby wild areas, exploring the natural wonders of her new home.

Mary's newfound passion for Alaska wildlife was soon put to good purpose. Not long after she moved to Fairbanks, she joined the Alaska Conservation Society, the state's first environmental organization, which had been founded in 1960 by Ginny Wood, Celia Hunter, and others (see previous chapter). The first project Mary helped with was the effort to purchase the historic Creamer's Field, a former dairy farm in Fairbanks, and establish it as a migratory waterfowl refuge. As a Campfire Girls leader, Mary and her Bluebird troop held a bake sale to raise funds for the project. In 1968 the 2,000-acre farm became Creamer's Field Migratory Wildlife Refuge.

During her first two years in Fairbanks, Mary began to dream of a different experience—to live in a cabin in the wilderness. In 1968, as autumn was approaching, she and a friend found a small abandoned cabin halfway between Fairbanks and Anchorage, less than a hundred miles south of the entrance to Mount McKinley National Park (now Denali National Park). She contacted the owner, who gave the young women permission to use the cabin over the winter. At the last minute, the friend took a job in the Yukon, leaving Mary on her own. Although she was "a little uncertain about living in the wilds by myself," she recalled, "my heart was set on the adventure so off I went. This simple decision changed my life." At the cabin she would learn—mostly by trial and error—many of the skills she would need for her future life in the wilderness.

On a golden September day, Mary stepped off the train with boxes of winter supplies and trudged to her new home at the base of Chulitna Butte. When she reached the spot, she saw that the cabin she'd viewed only at a distance from the train was "more than rustic, more than run-down." Undaunted, she spent the next few days fixing up the cabin, chasing off the porcupines that had taken up residence, cleaning out the mess, and doing repairs on the place she dubbed "the Last Resort." Compensating for the cabin's deficiencies was its view of the Great One, Mount McKinley, North America's highest peak.

As the weeks passed, Mary was finding it difficult to drag in all her water and firewood by herself. Furthermore, if she needed supplies, she had to trudge through the snow and flag down the train to get to the nearest town, Gold Creek, thirteen miles to the south. These problems were unexpectedly solved after some friends from Fairbanks, Mike and Sally Jones, visited Mary at the cabin in October and offered to lend her a sled and three of their dogs. Saying yes was another fateful decision for Mary. Three days later at the train tracks, the baggage man handed down to her an old gray sled, several fifty-pound bags of dog food, and three excited huskies. Her friends had written her a note with the dogs' names: Kiana, Rusty, and Agean. "Dear Mary, Good luck!" the note said. "Just harness them up and away you'll go!" But it was not, she quickly discovered, that simple.

Mary had no idea how to harness the dogs, much less command them. After fumbling her way through tying the animals to the sled, she called out "Mush, you malamutes!" The dogs pulled in all directions, ending up in a tangle of ropes, legs, and tails. She finally let the dogs loose to follow her as she herself dragged the loaded sled back to the cabin.

Upon reaching home, Mary unloaded the dog food and fed the dogs, then tried the sled again. She found that hitching up one dog at a time, rather than all three at once, helped her and the dogs ease into the learning process. By evening, she had driven each of the three dogs to a nearby creek and back. Within a day or two, she and her team had gotten the hang of things. There was no doubt that having dogs who could pull twenty-gallon water jugs uphill from the creek made Mary's life in the wilderness much easier. But more than that, she learned how much she liked the warm companionship her furry new friends provided. "Over the winter," Mary later wrote, "the country taught me many lessons. . . . I had time to watch and listen. . . . A peace filled me and gave me strength I had not known before."

By February, Mary's money was running low, so she decided to go to Valdez, east of Anchorage, for a while to work as a nurse's aide in the hospital there. She left Rusty and Agean with neighbors and took Kiana with her to Valdez. A month later she happily returned to the cabin and settled back in with her canine companions. One day Mary noticed that Kiana, the female, was getting a bit fat around the belly. Sure enough, a few weeks later, Mary discovered six black pups with Kiana in her dog shelter. The puppies bore a striking resemblance to the black labrador that Mary had seen hanging around the gas station in Valdez.

All winter, Mary had been planning an early-spring sled trek through McKinley Park. She had never seen the park under snow, and she was determined not to let the new arrivals interfere with the trip. Packing up the sled and gathering the three adult dogs and all six pups, she took the train to the park entrance. There she tied her gear onto the sled, nestled the box of puppies toward the back where she could watch them, harnessed the three team dogs, and took off up the main road. She arranged to stay in a ranger cabin on the Savage River, from which point she could take day trips through the park. To her delight, she found that the distance she was able to mush increased each day.

In May, Mary was back at the winter cabin, packing up to leave. Before starting a summer job, she needed to find homes for the pups, who were now weaned. She took them to Talkeetna, where she quickly found takers for five of them. But one, a plump, black puppy she had nicknamed Cabbage, was left. When Mary went to Fairbanks to return Kiana, Rusty, and Agean to the Joneses, little Cabbage was still with her. She soon realized that, whether or not she was ready to have a dog of her own, this round little mixed-breed was going to be hers to keep.

Back in Fairbanks in June, Mary again stayed with the Lawlors, her former employers, but she wanted a house of her own. The family gave her permission to build a cabin on their property, and she energetically set to work. The finished product was not exactly an architectural wonder, but it served its purpose for a time. During her next two years in Fairbanks, Mary enrolled for classes at the University of Alaska and worked at various jobs for income. Whenever possible, she borrowed a neighbor's sled dogs for quick runs or accompanied friends on trips with their teams, along with Cabbage, who was learning to be a sled dog himself.

In November 1971, at a friend's ice-skating party, Mary met John Manthei, a researcher at the Institute of Arctic Biology who was studying vegetation along the route of the proposed trans-Alaska pipeline. While chatting, the two discovered, to their mutual surprise, that they had grown up in towns only twenty-five miles apart in Wisconsin. John had moved to Alaska the previous year because Wisconsin, he felt, was too crowded. Like Mary, he had fallen deeply in love with the Northland wilderness.

A short time later, Mary asked John to go on a "sledding picnic" with her. They borrowed a friend's dogs for the day trip. Their friendship grew closer, and Mary admitted to being "a little starry-eyed whenever he was around." In March 1972, while John was gone on a solo six-week trip into the Brooks Range, Mary was invited to join three friends on an expedition to Wonder Lake. It was her first deep-wilderness sledding excursion, and she learned much about mushing and winter camping from her more-experienced companions. Mary was proud of Cabbage, now three years old, who she said "tugged along pulling his fair share." Increasingly passionate about dogsledding, Mary vowed that by the next winter, she would have a team of her own.

By the fall of 1972, Mary indeed had her dog team. Her friends Mike and Sally Jones had given her Kiana, Cabbage's mother, to keep, as well as two of her recent pups, Ambler and Kobuk. Another friend gave her four-month-old Luna, the "moon dog." Along with her own faithful Cabbage, Mary now had five dogs, enough for a serviceable sled team. She spent weeks training the dogs to pull together on the trail, trying different combinations of dogs in different positions and getting them ready for longer and longer trips.

Mary was teaching at a Fairbanks elementary school that year, and when the snows came, she began sledding to work with her dogs. After school, she and her team would hit the trail and run for hours. Mary spent most of her weekends with John, taking overnight sled trips to various spots.

In March 1973, John and Mary embarked on a monthlong adventure into the Alaska Range. They traveled over packed trails, deep loose snow, and frozen rivers. At times the temperature dipped to forty degrees below zero, and more than once the pair became lost. But good or bad, Mary and John relished every minute.

At the same time John and Mary were on their trip, a new event was taking place in Alaska—the first Iditarod Trail Sled Dog Race. Contestants ran a grueling 1,000-plus-mile course from Anchorage to Nome, mushing through tundra, woods, mountains, and rivers while enduring frigid temperatures, gale-force winds, and blizzards. Alaskans loved it. The first race was so successful, the organizers decided to hold it every year.

After a long sledding excursion with John over the holidays of 1973–74, Mary began to dream of entering the next Iditarod race. After all, she and her dogs had made it through several long and strenuous wilderness sled trips—why not try a new challenge?

The contest rules set the minimum number of dogs at eight. Mary bought three more dogs, Snowflake, Ole, and Morgan, giving her an eligible team. Cabbage would be the lead dog. She trained the animals vigorously for the few weeks she had left before the Iditarod's March 4 start.

Participating in the Iditarod was an expensive proposition. In addition to the entry fee was the cost of supplies—extra-warm clothing, food rations, dog food, snowshoes, camping gear, and many other items. To help Mary with these expenses, her Fairbanks friends and neighbors held a benefit potluck. In addition, the dogs needed booties to protect their feet when trail conditions were rough. Most of these booties were hand-sewn by volunteers in Anchorage and donated to the mushers. Someone had embroidered one bundle of booties with little cabbages in honor of Mary's dog Cabbage. Touched, she kept some of these as souvenirs after the race.

On the morning of the race, forty-three mushers and their teams took their places as dozens of spectators stood ready to cheer them on. Mary's team of eight dogs was the smallest in the race. Many of the contestants were running the race for the second time, eager to try again for the first-place purse of $12,000. But unlike the first Iditarod, in which all the contenders were men, this one included two female mushers, Mary and a woman named Lolly Medley. Among the crowd were murmurs about the women racers; many people thought they'd never make it to Nome. Hearing these naysayers only fired Mary's (and Lolly's) determination to prove them wrong.

By afternoon on the first day, the five teams who had earlier been behind Mary had passed her, and she was in last place. But as the sky darkened, her dogs, who liked traveling at night, began pulling faster, and she started to catch up with and pass other teams. Mary noted that often the other racers seemed perturbed when they saw that the musher passing them was a woman. When she stopped at 1:00 a.m. to camp for a few hours at the first checkpoint at Knik, sixty miles from Anchorage, she was pleased to find that she'd moved up to twenty-sixth place.

A ten-day spell of extreme cold and high winds slowed all the racers down. Later, a heavy snowfall impeded their progress, often forcing the mushers to stop and break new trail on snowshoes. Providing welcome breaks from these struggles, however, were residents of villages along the route who offered the mushers hot coffee and hot food as well as warm encouragement. When she reached the Yukon, halfway to Nome, Mary learned that people were making bets on whether Mary and Lolly would be scratched from the race. "As we continued from checkpoint to checkpoint," Mary recalled, "women were backing us and winning their bets."

As Mary labored along the trail, talking and singing encouragement to her dogs as they plodded forward, she savored the sensual bounty around her. She was thrilled at the sight of the Northern Lights, comforted by the fresh aroma of the pine trees, and lulled by the sound of the sled's runners whooshing and the dogs' panting through an otherwise silent landscape. At the last checkpoint before the sea-ice crossing to Nome, Mary stopped for a quick rest. When she awoke, she found that Lolly had pulled out ahead of her. Urging her team on double-time, Mary reached Nome in the early morning hours and discovered she had beat Lolly after all.

At the finish line, despite the predawn hour, Mary was greeted with hearty cheers, flashing camera bulbs, and blaring sirens. The wife of Nome's mayor presented Mary with a bouquet of roses. Although twenty-two teams had reached Nome ahead of her, Mary had made history as the first woman ever to finish the race. About half an hour later, Lolly Medley crossed the finish line, causing another eruption of cheers and sirens. The two women were offered Nome's best hotel suite, furnished with flowers, fresh fruit baskets, and champagne. The welcome, Mary later wrote, "is a memory dear to my heart."

A few days later, in a surprise move, Mary turned her team around and mushed her dogs back toward Anchorage along the same route. On the way, she stopped in at the various villages to thank the residents for their hospitality. She made it as far as Galena, but due to melting snow she had to take a plane the last five hundred miles to Fairbanks.

While this Iditarod was the only one that Mary would compete in, it was not her last dogsled race. Over the next few years she would participate in many contests, including the formidable Yukon Quest.

When Mary arrived back in Fairbanks and returned to her rickety cabin, she found a note from John. "Welcome back, M! I'm out at the creek, cutting logs for the cabin." The year before, John had purchased some roadless land about thirty miles west of Fairbanks, in the Goldstream Valley, to build a new cabin for the two of them. While Mary was gone, he had felled some fifty trees and he was now busy cutting them to size. Mary and her dogs jumped right in to help with the hauling. By the fall, the one-room cabin was complete with a sod roof, windows, and a door. Just in time for winter, John bought an old, five-hundred-pound cast-iron stove for cooking and heat. The stove was so heavy, John had to build a new, stronger sled to move it. Once the home was ready, John and Mary set to work building shelters for the dogs—"doggie duplexes," they called them. Mary cut long grass from along the creek to make sweet-smelling hay beds for the doghouses.

John and Mary's fourteen-by-fourteen-foot cabin was cozy but rustic—just the way they liked it. Oil lamps provided light, and a nearby spring-fed creek was their water supply. Perishable food was stored in an enclosed space beneath the cabin floor, where year-round temperatures stayed just above freezing. Each year, the two added a few more more amenities to their wilderness hideaway.

John and Mary's goal was to live in their cabin year-round, but it would be nearly seven years before they could afford to do that. In the meantime, they would live and work in Fairbanks during the week and spend the weekends in their dream home. Each of them had a cabin near town, but John asked Mary if it wouldn't make more sense for them to share a place. As he put it, "It's silly for both of us to cut wood for two cabins." She agreed. "It was not the first time I had considered the idea," she later wrote, "although not exactly in terms of firewood."

During this period, Mary worked for the state government in the Department of Fish and Game, and John continued at the university. For the next several years, while the couple lived in Fairbanks, the wilderness cabin served as their headquarters for sledding excursions. Finally, in the fall of 1980, John and Mary were ready to move in permanently. John had built a woodworking shop beside the cabin, where he could do custom cabinetry and furniture for income. Mary settled in and began polishing her writing skills. Four years later, her first book, *Sled Dog Trails*, was published. Her poetic follow-up, *Small Wonders: Year-Round Alaska*, based on her own nature journal, was published in 1987. The book was dedicated to "the black-capped and boreal chickadees—small wonders that sing even at forty degrees below zero."

Meanwhile, sledding travels with her dogs still occupied much of Mary's life. In 1983 she heard about a new cross-country sled race to be held in February 1984, plans for which were under way. Organized by a group of Fairbanks mushers, the Yukon Quest International Sled Dog Race was created in honor of the historical Yukon River Trail used by travelers to and from the Klondike

Mary's memoirs, *Sled Dog Trails*, published in 1984
—Courtesy Mary Shields

goldfields at the turn of the twentieth century. The route would follow 1,000 miles of the old trail, starting in Fairbanks and ending in
Whitehorse, Yukon Territory, Canada.

A few years earlier, Mary had sledded to Dawson City, Yukon Territory, with John, using much of the same route the racers would
follow. Certainly it would be fun to enter this race, Mary thought, but
even more appealing was the organizers' dedication to "excellence

in canine care" and "fostering the traditions of northern travel by dog sled." Both of these ideals were deeply important to Mary. Thus, February found Mary Shields and her eight dogs among the twenty-six teams lining up in Fairbanks for the first annual Yukon Quest race.

In some ways, the Yukon Quest was more challenging than the Iditarod, Mary felt. It started a month earlier, in February, when the weather can be extremely cold. There were fewer checkpoints,

Mary Shields just before her first Yukon Quest race, February 1984 —Courtesy Mary Shields

including one section where stops were two hundred miles apart. The trail, which often ran on the frozen Yukon River itself, also crossed four mountain summits. Due to the danger, the racers adopted a motto, "Survival first, race second." On the plus side for Mary, the Yukon Quest was better suited than the Iditarod for her one-hundred-pound dogs, who were heavier and slower, but steadier and sturdier, than many of the other racers' dogs, who were bred for speed. In any case, for Mary, the race was not about winning so much as it was "a personal challenge to gain a deeper understanding of this vast land."

After approximately two weeks on the trail, twenty teams, including Mary's, crossed the finish line in Fairbanks; six had dropped out. With a time of fourteen days, seventeen hours, and nineteen minutes, Mary placed sixteenth. The winning time was twelve days and five minutes. Loving the experience, Mary entered the Yukon Quest again in 1986 and 1988. The 1986 race was her best; she finished in eleventh place and won $900. In 1988 she again placed sixteenth with a time almost exactly the same as in 1984—fourteen days, seventeen hours, and fifteen minutes.

The summer after her first Yukon Quest, Mary began a new venture that let her show off her dogs and demonstrate mushing to tourists. A Fairbanks tour company, Riverboat Discovery, which had been popular with visitors to Alaska since 1950, gave Mary a spot on their tour in 1984. Several times a day, the tour's triple-deck paddleboat dropped anchor on the north bank of the Tanana River and the passengers disembarked near Mary's cabin. Mary would meet her guests with a hearty greeting and show them around the property as she regaled them with tales of her snowy exploits. The visitors then watched in fascination as she hitched up her team and mushed them along a short gravel trail. Mary, who delighted in the visits, continued working for Riverboat Discovery every summer for the next eleven years.

Not long after Mary began working with Riverboat Discovery, she and John were married. In 1988 Mary made a film about her life with her dogs. The hour-long documentary, *Season of the Sled Dog*, aired on public broadcasting; Mary also sold copies on her own. Narrated by Mary herself, the movie depicts her and John's life in their backwoods cabin and reveals how she and her team negotiate snowy trails. She notes that most sled dogs are not purebred huskies or malemutes, but mixtures bred for various traits, depending on the musher's needs. She shows and discusses the dogs' thick coats and big, sturdy paws. Apparent throughout the film is the joy Mary feels mushing with and caring for her dogs, which in 1988 included Little Joe, Jack, Schnitzel, Solo, Uproar, Flopsy, and seven others. Mary wanted to make the movie as a way to show viewers "how useful a dog team is, and what admirable personalities the dogs have."

As much as Mary and John loved their remote cabin and the surrounding wilderness, it was becoming impractical to remain so far away from Fairbanks. Living closer to town, they would be able to install power and phone lines and have easier access to stores for supplies. So in 1989, the couple built a larger and more modern log cabin on twenty wooded acres with road access to Fairbanks. Still in their beloved Goldstream Valley, the new place was only twelve miles from town instead of thirty. Best of all, the new home had indoor plumbing.

Mary continued her summer program for Riverboat Discovery until 1994. Sadly, around that time, she and John separated. She remained in the large cabin while John moved into his own cabin. Today he teaches woodworking in Fairbanks.

In 1995 Mary decided that, since she now had a telephone and electricity, she could establish her own business. She would conduct tours similar to those she had given for Riverboat Discovery, but longer and with much smaller groups so that she and her guests could "get to know each other." During the program, called "Tails of the Trail," Mary introduced guests to her dogs and demonstrated how she harnessed them, drove the sled, and set up a winter camp. With the smaller groups, she was able to take visitors inside her cabin for refreshments (her brownies were especially popular) while she told stories of her mushing experiences. Mary's tours became increasingly popular as the years passed, and she still hosts Tails of the Trail to this day. In 2013 the Fairbanks Chamber of Commerce chose Mary as the winner of their Golden Heart Award for "exceptional hospitality and commitment to visitors."

Mary particularly enjoyed her younger guests, and she wanted them to understand the importance of the role sled dogs play in bush Alaska. In fact, she wanted to share her appreciation for these animals with all children, so in the early 1990s she wrote a series of nonfiction books for kids she dubbed "the Happy Dog Trilogy." *Can Dogs Talk?* was published in 1991, *Loving a Happy Dog* in 1992, and *Secret Messages: Training a Happy Dog* in 1993.

Meanwhile, another racing opportunity presented itself, and it was one Mary could not resist. The Hope Race was designed as a goodwill event between the United States and Russia in the wake of the fall of the Soviet Union. In the inaugural race, to be held on April 4, 1991, mushers would traverse 1,200 miles from Nome to Anadyr, Siberia. The event's three organizers—artist Jon Van Zyle of Eagle River, Leo Rasmusson of Nome, and Jerry Tokor of Anchorage—planned the event as an international contest, in which teams of mushers from several countries would compete against Chukchi mushers from Siberia. Participation was by invitation only. Mary was one of only three Americans to be chosen to compete. According to Van Zyle, "She best represented the idealism and focus of what the Hope Race could be."

Fourteen teams—seven from each side of the Bering Strait—would be competing. The United States sponsored an international team composed of one Swiss, one Japanese, one Norwegian, one

Canadian, and three American mushers. Among the Americans were two women, Mary and Kotzebue musher Kate Persons. Seven Chukchi mushers would represent Russia.

On the day of the race, Mary and her eight-dog team took their place among the six other international mushers in Nome. Because Russia would not allow the Chukchi mushers to start the race on the American side of the Bering Strait, they would be meeting their rivals in Uelin, Siberia. The U.S.-sponsored teams planned to cross the icy strait from Wales, Alaska, into Siberia, but when they reached Wales, the ice was deemed too thin to cross. After waiting four days for conditions to improve, Russia sent military helicopters to transport the American teams to the Siberian coast. "They just landed in Wales, opened the helicopter hatch, and we drove the teams right aboard," Mary recalled.

Giving local kids sled rides in Wales, Alaska —Courtesy Mary Shields

In Russia, Mary found the Chukchis to be "all so very kind" and noted that they had a "whole different way of sledding. Mushers sat on their sleds and traveled side by side so they could talk." When the contestants stopped to rest, the Siberian villagers would give them the most comfortable bed in the house. Despite their difficult lives, the Siberians shared whatever they had, serving pots of reindeer stew to the mushers at stops along the trail.

After five weeks on the trail, Mary reached Anadyr in mid-May, crossing the finish line in about eleventh or twelfth place, she said. The winner was Kate Persons, a fact that pleased Mary. "She had a beautiful team and a beautiful smile and was a great ambassador for the United States," Mary remarked. After the race, the Siberians treated all the contestants to a banquet that featured entertainment by Native dancers. Several of the U.S.-sponsored mushers remained in Siberia for another week or so to enjoy the local spring festivals. Mary called the Hope Race, her last long-distance competition, a "once in a lifetime experience."

With her racing career behind her, Mary hoped to find more time to devote to environmental concerns. Her goal as a conservationist was to protect the wonders of the natural world for future generations. "I appreciate how much the wilderness has given me," she said, "and I want to work so that others can enjoy it as I have."

In 1999, to protect her own Goldstream Valley property from further development in the future, Mary donated a twenty-acre conservation easement to the Interior Alaska Land Trust. In the terms of the donation, typical for an easement, Mary retained the right to keep living on the land, and the land trust agreed to keep the property, with its impressive old-growth forest, in a relatively undisturbed condition in perpetuity. "This old forest has taught me many things—most importantly, the patience to stay in one place and know that place intimately," Mary stated. ". . . I ask the Interior Alaska Land Trust to care for this forest in the future, so others may also come here and watch and listen and feel and learn and love."

In 2005 Mary participated in a rally organized by Alaskans Protecting the Arctic Refuge. Also in attendance was Ginny Wood. At the same time, Mary continued her involvement with the Northern Alaska Environmental Center (NAEC), serving on its board of directors for six years in the 2000s. Among the center's goals were protecting wildlife habitats and encouraging the development of clean, renewable energy sources. Mary also served on the center's Clean Water and Mining Program committee, whose aim was to see that Alaska's mines complied with environmental protection regulations. In 2009 the NAEC presented Mary with its Conservationist of the Year Award "for her outstanding leadership on climate change education and advocacy in the Interior."

As a member of a group called Clean Air Fairbanks in 2011, Mary helped sponsor the Healthy Air Protection Act, a citizen initiative to restrict wintertime wood burning to protect the city's air quality. In support of the initiative, she wrote: "On many winter days, we have unhealthy and even hazardous smoke pollution. As a wood burner who has long heated with an indoor stove, I burn responsibly and efficiently without excessive smoke. That's not too much to ask when the lives of our residents are at risk. . . . We all live here expecting to have our basic needs met: clean water and clean air. . . . [We voters] have a responsibility to do all we can to safeguard these basic needs for all the residents of our community. "

As of early 2014, the battle against pollution in Fairbanks continues. "If what we're doing is harming children's health," she declared at a recent community meeting, "we should be ashamed of ourselves."

Mary's contributions to the sport of dog mushing have been extolled in numerous articles and books over the years. In 1995 she was presented with Mush with Pride's first annual Lifetime Achievement Award. In 2010 she was invited to be the keynote speaker at the Willow Dog Mushers Association's Mushing History Conference and K9 Athletes Symposium. In addition, she partici-

Mary at home with one of her best friends, 2011 —Courtesy Mary Shields

pated in a panel called "Pioneering Women Mushers and Their K9 Athletes" during the statewide conference. The event also featured a screening of Mary's 1988 film, *Season of the Sled Dog.*

Today there are only five dogs in Mary's yard, two of which are getting on in years. At age seventy, Mary continues to live alone on her beloved homestead, welcoming her Tails of the Trail summer visitors as well as friends throughout the year. She also writes an annual newsletter to keep friends and former tour guests apprised on how she and her dogs are faring. In closing her 2013 newsletter, Mary wrote, "Listen to the north wind after dinner and you will hear my pals howling their good night. And if you hear one little alto, slightly off key, well, that will be me. Good Night and Good Winter." It was signed "Too Sweet, O.J., Crockett, Frosty-Frosty, Big Boy, and Mary."

Selected Bibliography

1. NATALIA SHELIKHOVA

Black, Dawn Lea, and Alexander Yu Petrov. *Natalia Shelikova, Russian Oligarch of Alaska Commerce*. Fairbanks: University of Alaska Press, 2010.

Black, Lydia T. *Russians in Alaska, 1732–1867*. Fairbanks: University of Alaska Press, 2004.

Chevigny, Hector. *Russian America*. New York: Viking Press, 1965.

Grauman, Melody W. "Women and Culture in Russian America." *American West* 11:3 (May 1974).

Naske, Claus M., and Herman E. Slotnick. *Alaska: A History of the 49th State*. Grand Rapids, Mich.: William B. Eerdmans Publishing, 1979.

Oliver, James A. *The Bering Strait Crossing*. Np: Information Architects, 2006.

Petrov, Dr. Alexander, and Dawn Lea Black. *Natalia Shelikov: Her Unique and Influential Involvement in the Mercantile and Imperial Russian Arenas*. Pdf. http://www.fortross.org/lib/117/natalia-shelikov-her-unique-and-influential-involvement-in-the-mercantile-and-imperial-russian-arenas.pdf.

2. MARY ANTISARLOOK

Brooks, Maria. *The Reindeer Queen*. Film. Preview: http://www.der.org/films/reindeer-queen.html.

Brown, Tricia. "Sinrock Mary: Mary Antisarlook. LitSite Alaska." http://www.litsite.org/index.cfm?section=Digital-Archives&page=People-of-the-North&cat=Native-Lives-and-Traditions&viewpost=2&Contentld=2564.

Lopp-Smith, Kathleen. *Ice Window: Letters from a Bering Strait Village, 1898–1902*. Fairbanks: University of Alaska Press, 2001.

Olson, Dean F. *Alaska Reindeer Herdmen*. http://www.alaskool.org/projects/reindeer/history/iser1969/rdeer_1.html.

Ray, Dorothy Jean. "Sinrock Mary: From Eskimo Wife to Reindeer Queen." *Pacific Northwest Quarterly* 75 (1984).

———. *Eskimos of the Bering Strait, 1650–1898.* Seattle: University of Washington Press, 1975.

"Sinrock Mary." Wikipedia. http://en.wikipedia.org/wiki/Sinrock_Mary.

"Sinrock Mary: Reindeer Queen." http://library.thinkquest.org/11313/Early_History/Native_Alaskans/mary.html.

Taliaferro, John. *In a Far Country: The True Story of a Mission, a Marriage, a Murder, and the Remarkable Reindeer Rescue of 1898.* New York: Public Affairs, 2006.

U.S. Bureau of Education. *Annual Report to Congress on the Introduction of Domestic Reindeer into Alaska, 1894.* Vol. 13. Washington, DC: Government Printing Office, 1904.

Willis, Roxanne. *A New Game in the North: Native Reindeer Herding, 1890–1940.* http://www.foresthistory.org/fellowships/willis.pdf

Zagoskin, Lavrenty A. *Lieutenant Zagoskin's Travels in Russian America, 1842–1844.* Ed. Henry N. Michael. Toronto: University of Toronto Press, 1967.

3. RUSTY DOW

"Alaska Highway." Wikipedia. http://en.wikipedia.org/wiki/Alaska_Highway.

Dow, Benzie Ola "Rusty." Papers. Consortium Library Archives and Special Collections, University of Alaska, Anchorage. https://consortiumlibrary.org/archives/CollectionsList/CollectionDescriptions/hmc-0397cd.html.

Dow, Russell. Papers. Consortium Library Archives and Special Collections, University of Alaska, Anchorage.

Gilman, William. "Ladies Cannot Work in Skirts, Insists Rusty Dow, Handsome Girl Sourdough." *Milwaukee Journal,* March 12, 1942. http://news.google.com/newspapers?nid=1499&dat=19420312&id=vPQZAAAAIBAJ&sjid=diMEAAAAIBAJ&pg=3298,4960196.

Jones, Cherry Lyon. "Benzie Ola 'Rusty' Dow." In *More Than Petticoats: Remarkable Alaska Women.* Guilford, Conn.: Morris Book Publishing (Globe Pequot Press), 2006.

Project 49: Benzie Ola "Rusty" Dow. University of Alaska, Anchorage. http://greenandgold.uaa.alaska.edu/blog/20551/project-49-benzie-ola-rusty-dow-dean-women-war-workers-alaska/.

Sarasota Herald-Tribune. "First Woman to Drive Truck Over Alcan Highway . . ." January 31, 1947. http://news.google.com/newspapers?nid=1755&dat=19470131&id=QeIcAAAAIBAJ&sjid=n2QEAAAAIBAJ&pg=2974,2500803.

U.S. Army Corps of Engineers. "Historical Vignette 082—A: Female Corps Truck Driver Mastered the Alaska Wilderness." March 2004. http://www.usace.army.mil/About/History/HistoricalVignettes/WomenMinorities/082FemaleTruckDriver.aspx.

4. BARRETT WILLOUGHBY

"Barrett Willoughby." Wikipedia. http://en.wikipedia.org/wiki/Barrett_Willoughby

Ferrell, Nancy Warren. *Barrett Willoughby: Alaska's Forgotten Lady.* Fairbanks: University of Alaska Press, 1994.

Spawn of the North (film). Wikipedia. http://en.wikipedia.org/wiki/Spawn_of_the_North.

Willoughby, Barrett. "Ben Eielson: Pioneer of the Arctic Skies." In *Alaskans All.* Boston: Houghton Mifflin, 1933.

———. "A Little Alaskan Schooner Was My Childhood Home." In *American Magazine*, October 1924.

———. *Sitka: Portal to Romance.* Boston: Houghton Mifflin, 1930.

———. "A Trail Blazer's Adventures at the Top of the World." In *Gentlemen Unafraid.* New York: G. P. Putnam's Sons, 1928.

———. *Where the Sun Swings North.* New York: G. P. Putnam's Sons, 1922.

5. ELIZABETH PERATROVICH

"AlaskaNativeBrotherhood/Sisterhood."Wikipedia.http://en.wikipedia.org/wiki/Alaska_Native_Brotherhood/Sisterhood.

Alaskool.org. "A Recollection of Civil Rights Leader Elizabeth Peratrovich, 1911–1958." http://www.alaskool.org/projects/native_gov/recollections/peratrovich/elizabeth_1.htm.

Dauenhauer, Nora Marks, and Richard Dauenhauer, eds. *Haa Kusteeyi, Our Culture: Tlingit Life Stories.* Seattle: University of Washington Press, 1994.

Dunham, Mike. "Tlingit Civil Rights Pioneer Celebrated in Film." *Anchorage Daily News*, October 17, 2009. http://www.adn.com/2009/10/17/977688/tlingit-civil-rights-pioneer-celebrated.html.

"Elizabeth Peratrovich." Wikipedia. http://en.wikipedia.org/wiki/ Elizabeth_Peratrovich.

Kiffer, Dave. "Alaska Celebrates Civil Rights Pioneer." SitNews, Ketchikan, Alaska, February 18, 2008. http://www.sitnews.us/Kiffer/ Peratrovich/021808_e_peratrovich.html.

Murkowski, Sen. Lisa. U.S. Congressional Record S. 2900 (October 6, 2004). http://thomas.loc.gov/cgi-bin/query/z?c108:S.2900.IS:.

Sterling, Libby. "Battle for Brotherhood: Alaskans Remember the Peratroviches." *Capital City Weekly*, February 11, 2009. http://www. capitalcityweekly.com/stories/021109/new_386889227.shtml.

Tetpon, John. "In Memory of a Rights Advocate." *Anchorage Daily News*, June 6, 1988. http://www.alaskool.org/projects/ancsa/articles/ ADN/Peratrovich_Day.htm.

Ulmer, Rep. Fran. "Honoring Elizabeth Wanamaker Peratrovich." May 1, 1992. University of Alaska Anchorage. http://www.uaa.alaska. edu/spotlight/franulmer/honoring-elizabeth-peratrovich.cfm.

Williams, Van. "Keeping the Peratrovich Legend Alive." First Alaskans Institute newsletter, April/May 2010.

6. Mahala Ashley Dickerson

Alaska Friends. "Mahala Ashley Dickerson." *Epistle of Alaska Friends Conference Annual Session*, September 2002. Pdf. http://www. pacificyearlymeeting.org/wordpress/wp-content/uploads/2013/08/ AlaskaEpistle2012.pdf.

American Bar Association. "Mahala Ashley Dickerson." Pdf. http:// www.americanbar.org/content/dam/aba/migrated/women/bios/ mahala_dickerson.authcheckdam.pdf.

Associated Press. "Pioneering Alaska lawyer dies at 94." *Juneau Empire*, February 22, 2007. http://juneauempire.com/stories/022207/ sta_20070222010.shtml.

Dickerson, M. Ashley. *Delayed Justice for Sale*. Anchorage: Al-Acres, Inc., 1991.

Hammons, Helen. "Alabama Legal Pioneer Dies in Alaska." http://www. wsfa.com/story/6121740/alabama-legal-pioneer-dies-in-alaska.

Harmon, David. "Mahala Ashley Dickerson." *Encyclopedia of Alabama*. http://en.wikipedia.org/wiki/Mahala_Ashley_Dickerson.

————. "Montgomery Industrial School for Girls." *Encyclopedia of Alabama*. http://www.encyclopediaofalabama.org/face/Article.jsp?id=h-1162.

"Mahala Ashley Dickerson." Wikipedia. http://en.wikipedia.org/wiki/ Mahala_Ashley_Dickerson.

7. CELIA HUNTER AND GINNY HILL WOOD

Alaska Conservation Foundation. "Celia Hunter, 1919–2001." http:// alaskaconservation.org/foundation/history-founders/celia-hunter/.

Alaska Women's Hall of Fame. "Celia Hunter." http://alaskawomenshall offame.org/2011/02/28/celia-hunter/.

Alaska Women's Hall of Fame. "Virginia 'Ginny' Hill Wood." http://alaska womenshalloffame.org/2011/02/28/virginia-ginny-hill-wood/.

Barlow, Connie. "Celia Hunter, Wilderness Advocate." Tribute, December 2013. http://www.thegreatstory.org/celia-hunter.html.

Branch, Maureen Conley. "Interview with Virginia Hill Wood." Veterans History Project. Fairbanks, Alaska, March 17, 2004. http:// lcweb2.loc.gov/diglib/vhp/story/loc.natlib.afc2001001.12670/ transcript?ID=sr0001.

Brewster, Karen, ed. *Boots, Bikes, and Bombers: Adventures of Alaska Conservationist Ginny Hill Wood.* Fairbanks: University of Alaska Press, 2012.

Brinkley, Douglas. *The Quiet World: Saving Alaska's Wilderness Kingdom, 1879-1960.* New York: HarperCollins, 2011.

Caddell, Amy. "Virginia 'Ginny' Hill Wood." http://www.findagrave.com/ cgi-bin/fg.cgi?page=gr&GRid=106451103.

Camp Denali Northface Lodge. "The Early Years." http://campdenali. com/live/page/our-history.

"Celia M. Hunter." Wikipedia. http://en.wikipedia.org/wiki/Celia_M._ Hunter.

Connelly, Joel. "Alaska loses Celia Hunter, one of its great ones." *Seattle Post-Intelligencer*, December 9, 2001.

Ellis, Tim. "Friends Recall the Life and Times of Legendary Alaskan Ginny Wood." http://fm.kuac.org/post/friends-recall-life-and-times-legendary-alaskan-ginny-wood.

"Ginny Wood." Wikipedia. http://en.wikipedia.org/wiki/Ginny_Wood.

Inslee, Rep. Jay. "Tribute to Celia Hunter." December 20, 2001. http:// capitolwords.org/date/2001/12/20/E2371-2_tribute-to-celia-hunter/.

Johnson, Susan Hackley. "Celia Hunter: Portrait of an Activist." *Alaska Journal*, Autumn 1979.

Los Angeles Times. "Ginny Wood dies at 95; pioneering Alaska environmentalist." March 12,2013. http://articles.latimes.com/2013/mar/12/local/la-me-ginny-wood-20130313.

Miller, Pamela. "Ginny Hill Wood, 95, passes on lasting wilderness legacy." Northern Alaska Environmental Center.

Murkowski, Sen. Lisa. "Remembering Virginia 'Ginny' Hill Wood." U.S. Congressional Record S. 2024 (March 20, 2013). Pdf. http://northern.org/media-library/document-archive/arctic/arctic-refuge/remembering-virginia-ginny-hill-wood-sen.-lisa-murkowski-march-20-2013/at_download/file.

O'Neill, Dan. *The Firecracker Boys.* New York: St. Martin's Press, 1994.

Parrish, Nancy. "Virginia 'Ginny' Hill Wood, 43-W-4 March 8, 2013." WASP Final Flight, WASP on the Web, Wings Across America. http://waspfinalflight.blogspot.com/2013/07/virginia-ginny-hill-wood-43-w-4-march-8.html.

Project Jukebox (University of Alaska Fairbanks Oral History Program). "Ginny Wood." Transcript of April 3, 1996, interview. Fairbanks Communities of Memory. http://jukebox.uaf.edu/site7/interviews/1908.

Seifert, Richard D. "Celia Hunter: A Brief Biography." http://ecotopia.org/ecology-hall-of-fame/celia-hunter/.

Simpson, Sherry. "Defenders of the Land." Pdf. *Alaska Magazine,* September 2002. http://s3.amazonaws.com/hoth.bizango/assets/10896/02.pdf.

Smetzer, Mary Beth. "World War II aviator, environmentalist Ginny Wood dies at 95." *Fairbanks Daily News Miner,* March 11, 2013. http://www.newsminer.com/news/local_news/article_b98c73ac-8a21-11e2-a0eb-001a4bcf6878.html.

Sumner, Sandi. *Women Pilots of Alaska.* Jefferson, NC: McFarland & Company, 2005.

Udall, Sen. Mark. "Tribute to Alaska's Celia Hunter." December 20, 2001. http://capitolwords.org/date/2001/12/20/E2379-3_tribute-to-alaskas-celia-hunter/.

Wilderness.net. "Celia Hunter: An Alaskan Preservation Pioneer." http://www.wilderness.net/NWPS/hunter.

Wilderness Society. "Celia Hunter." http://wilderness.org/bios/former-council-members/celia-hunter.

8. Nora Guinn

Alaska Women's Hall of Fame. "Nora Venes Guinn." http://alaskawomen shalloffame.org/2011/02/28/nora-venes-guinn/.

Blackman, Margaret B. *Sadie Brower Neakok*. Seattle: University of Washington Press, 1989.

Conn, Stephen. *Town Law and Village Law*. Anchorage: Justice Center, University of Alaska, 1982.

Cooke, Christopher R. "In Memoriam 2005: Nora Guinn." https://www.alaskabar.org/servlet/content/in_memoriam___.html.

"Nora Guinn." Wikipedia. http://en.wikipedia.org/wiki/Nora_Guinn.

Project Jukebox (University of Alaska Fairbanks Oral History Program). "In Loving Memory of Nora Venes Guinn." Pdf. http://jukebox.uaf.edu/site7/sites/default/files/documents/nora_guinn.pdf.

Project Jukebox (University of Alaska Fairbanks Oral History Program). "Judge Nora Guinn." http://jukebox.uaf.edu/site7/judge-nora-guinns-slideshow.

Rieger, Lisa. "Rural Courts in Alaska." *Journal of Contemporary Criminal Justice* 10:2 (May 1994).

9. Thelma Buchholdt

Alaska Women's Hall of Fame. "Thelma Buchholdt." http://alaskawomen shalloffame.org/2011/02/28/thelma-buchholdt/.

Allvoices. "Thelma Garcia Buchholdt." http://www.allvoices.com/contributed-news/7344353-memoirs-of-a-filipina-cultural-minority-who-made-history.

Anchorage Daily News. "Thelma Buchholdt." Obituary. November 7, 2007. http://www.legacy.com/obituaries/adn/obituary.aspx?pid=97462264.

Asian Journal. "Thelma Garcia Buchholdt, 1934–2007." November 17–20, 2007. http://www.ajdigitaledition.com/pdfs/PDF/2007_LA/2007_11_17/2007_LA_11_17_Sec-Cp%20%209.pdf.

Babao, Zena Sultana. "In Memory of Thelma Garcia Buchholdt." *Asian Journal San Diego*. Nd. http://asianjournalusa.com/in-memory-of-thelma-garcia-buchholdt-p3751-141.htm.

Buchholdt, Thelma. *Filipinos in Alaska, 1788–1958*. Anchorage: Aboriginal Press, 1996.

Filipino American National Historical Society. "Thelma Garcia Buchholdt." Obituary. http://www.fanhs17.com/obituary.htm.

Los Angeles Times. "Thelma Garcia Buchholdt, 73; former Alaskan legislator." Obituary, November 22, 2007. http://articles.latimes.com/2007/nov/22/local/me-passings22.s2.

"Thelma Buchholdt." Wikipedia. http://en.wikipedia.org/wiki/Thelma_Buchholdt.

"Thelma Garcia Buchholdt." Thelma Buchholdt Archives. http://www.thelmabuchholdt.com.

10. MARY SHIELDS

Freedman, Lew. *Father of the Iditarod: The Joe Redington Story.* Seattle: Epicenter Press, 1996.

———. *Iditarod Classics: Tales of the Trail Told by the Men and Women Who Race Across Alaska.* Seattle: Epicenter Press, 1992.

"Hope Race." Wikipedia. http://en.wikipedia.org/wiki/Hope_Race.

"Iditarod Trail Sled Dog Race." Wikipedia. http://en.wikipedia.org/wiki/Iditarod_Trail_Sled_Dog_Race.

"Mary Shields." http://www.menstuff.org/archives/shields.html.

Schneider, William, and Maria Statscewich. "Mary Shields." Interview, May 9, 2011. Project Jukebox (University of Alaska Fairbanks Oral History Program). http://jukebox.uaf.edu/site/interviews/mary-shields.

Season of the Sled Dog: An Adventure in Alaska Mushing. DVD. Pyrola Publishing, 1985.

Shields, Mary. "Dog Mushing with Mary Shields, Fairbanks, Alaska." Alaskan Tails of the Trail. http://www.maryshields.com.

———. *Sled Dog Trails.* Fairbanks, Alaska: Pyrola Publishing, 1984.

———. *Small Wonders: Year-Round Alaska.* Fairbanks, Alaska: Pyrola Publishing, 1987.

"Yukon Quest." Wikipedia. http://en.wikipedia.org/wiki/Yukon_Quest.

GENERAL REFERENCES

Alaska Women's Hall of Fame. http://alaskawomenshalloffame.org.

www.alaskool.org.

www.ancestry.com.

www.wikipedia.org

"Women in Alaska's History." http://library.thinkquest.org/11313/.

Index

and road to Palmer, 42; and skiing,
44; and Whittier Tunnel, 45; Barrett
Willoughby in, 60, 61; during World
War II, 43, 45
Anchorage Ad Hoc Committee of
Young Democrats, 143
Anchorage Daily News, 102
Anchorage Police Department, 100
Anchorage Ski Club, 43, 44
Anderson, Anton, 53
Andrewuk, Andrew, 33, 37
ANS. *See* Alaska Native Sisterhood
antidiscrimination bill, 3, 78, 79, 82, 84
Antisarlook, Charlie, 22, 25, 27, 31
Antisarlook, Mary, 1, 2, 19–38; adopted
children of, 1, 2, 27, 37; childhood of,
20–21; death of, 37; documentary
film about, 37; first husband of,
22, 31; generosity of, 2, 33, 38; and
gold rush, 2, 30; inheritance of,
31–32; languages spoken by, 20;
names of, 19; parents of, 20, 21; and
reindeer herding, 2, 27–28, 29, 30, 32,
33; Russian heritage of, 19, 20, 21;
second husband of, 33, 37; tattoos
of, 22; wealth of, 2, 31, 33, 37
Anton Anderson Memorial Tunnel
(Whittier Tunnel), 45, 52
Anvil Creek, 29
ANWR. *See* Arctic National Wildlife
Range (ANWR)
Arctic Alaska Travel Service
(Westours), 112–13
Arctic National Wildlife Range/Refuge
(ANWR), 3, 118, 119
Arctic Valley ski area, 44
Arlington, Wash., 105
Army Corps of Engineers, 45, 46, 120
Ashley, Erna, 90, 102
Ashley, Harriet, 90, 102
Ashley, Hattie Ethel Moss, 90
Ashley, John Augustine, 90, 94
Asian Alaskan Cultural Center, 147, 148
Asian-Pacific Women's Conference, 147
Athabaskan Indians, 121, 127
Atomic Energy Commission (AEC),
119, 120
Attu, 45

Baranof Hotel, 82
Baranov, Aleksander, 15, 17
Barrett, Florence. *See* Willoughby,
Barrett
Barrett, Florence Klink (mother), 55,
56, 57; after marriage to Charles
Willoughby, 59, 64, 65, 68, 69, 70
Barrett, Florence "Beau" (niece), 60, 69,
71, 72
Barrett, Frederick "Fred," 55
Barrett, Lawrence "Loll," 55, 56, 57, 59,
60, 61
Barrett, Martin, 55, 56, 57–58, 64
*Barrett Willoughby: Alaska's Forgotten
Lady*, 54
Barrington, Sydney, 64
Barrow, 29, 128, 133, 144; Point Barrow,
28, 29
Barrymore, John, 66
Bear (ship), 22, 24, 29
Beard, H. Margaret, 91
Beckwith, Frank, 95, 96
Bellingham, Wash., 75
Benson, Diane, 86
Bering, Vitus, 7
Bering Sea, 6, 8, 126, 129
Bering Strait, 167, 168
Berkeley, Calif., 71
Bethel, 3, 127, 128, 129–31, 133–36, 144
Bethel Community Services, 133, 134
Bootleggers Cove, 43, 45
Boots, Bikes, and Bombers, 125
Brentwood, Calif., 140
Brewster, Karen, 125
Brook, Maria, 37
Brookings Institution, 143
Brower, Sadie. *See* Neakok, Sadie Brower
Buchholdt, Chris, 142, 148
Buchholdt, Dylan, 142, 148
Buchholdt, Hans, 142, 148
Buchholdt, Jon, 4, 140–41, 142, 143
Buchholdt, Thelma Garcia, 3–4,
138–151; in Alaska legislature, 4,
145; and Alaska Eskimo Whaling
Commission, 147; and Alaska
Women's Hall of Fame, 151;
book by, 4, 148; in California,
141–42; childhood of, 3, 138–140;

MARJORIE COCHRANE, a former staff writer for newspapers in Alaska and Idaho, holds a journalism degree from the University of Oregon. Now retired, she makes her home on Washington's Long Beach Peninsula. She is the mother of five and the grandmother of seventeen.

Marjorie is the author of several previous books, including *Between Two Rivers: The Growth of Chugiak-Eagle River,* published by the Alaska Historical Commission Studies in History in 1982, and *Three Dogs, Two Mules, and a Reindeer: True Animal Adventures on the Alaska Frontier,* published by Mountain Press in 2010. In addition, her children's stories and feature articles have appeared in numerous publications throughout the Northwest.